Adventist
FAMILY TRADITIONS

to Bless Your Heart and Home

Making memories that last a lifetime

Céleste perrino Walker

ADVENTIST FAMILY TRADITIONS

Pacific Press® Publishing Association
Nampa, Idaho
Oshawa, Ontario, Canada
www.pacificpress.com

Edited by Bonnie Tyson-Flyn
Designed by Michelle C. Petz
All images c/o Photodisc, Inc. except cover: trail photo–Corel Corporation; inside pp. 42, 116, 125 Adobe Image Library; pp. 68, 78, 95, 131 Pacific Press

Copyright © 2002 by
Pacific Press® Publishing Association
Printed in the United States of America
All Rights Reserved

Additional copies of this book can be purchased online at www.AdventistBookCenter.com

ISBN 0-8163-1876-X

01 02 03 04 05 • 5 4 3 2 1

Contents

Introduction 5

- **Chapter 1:** Friday Evening — 9
- **Chapter 2:** The Friday-Evening Meal — 31
- **Chapter 3:** Sabbath Worship, Service, and Rest — 42
- **Chapter 4:** Sabbath Dinner — 51
- **Chapter 5:** Saturday Night (a.k.a. Game Night) — 68
- **Chapter 6:** Family Ties — 78
- **Chapter 7:** Camp Meeting — 95
- **Chapter 8:** Witnessing — 105
- **Chapter 9:** Family Vacations — 116
- **Chapter 10:** Family Worship — 125
- **Chapter 11:** Miscellaneous — 131

Recipe Index 142

DEDICATION

This book is dedicated with love

to my sister, Aimeé and her husband, Sung-gu Kang,

who are beginning their own

Adventist Family Traditions.

Introduction

Adventist family traditions are relatively new as traditions go, since Adventism as a religion has existed only for a century and a half. Nonetheless, some of our traditions are distinct and unique. They set us apart and mark us as a group of like believers. Some of these traditions are passed on from one generation to the next. Some of them are particular to an ethnic group, a region, or even a church body, but many of them are recognizable to anyone in the Church, regardless of origin.

Are these traditions important? I believe so. They accomplish two very special tasks. First, they bind us to God by reinforcing our relationship to Him in a pattern of continuity. Second, they bond us to each other in solidarity, giving us the shared experiences of a group having common goals, beliefs, and practices. Our traditions are important because they anchor us to the past and keep us secure against an unknown future. They provide stability in times of change and uncertainty.

"Family traditions give us a way to keep alive some good memories from the past and to build new memories with our children." —Ken Caviness

---

You could say that God began the first tradition when He instituted the Sabbath. Every seven days, humankind was to stop and think of God. They were to remember Creation and look forward to Redemption. They were to celebrate together their existence, God's blessings, and their hope for the future. Traditions are those things that bring us back. They put solid ground under our feet again. They are memories that draw us home and anchor us with their sameness.

When I first considered writing this book, I wondered if I was the best person for the job. After all, I did not grow up Adventist. I became an Adventist when I was nineteen. The traditions I celebrate with my family began after the birth of our children and are a mix of the old and the new. Some are taken from my family when I was growing up, others are borrowed from my husband Rob's family, and there are some unique to us as a family.

So I decided to ask you, fellow Adventists, for your traditions. The response was overwhelming. You sent your traditions from all over the world. I have been blessed by your traditions and have made many of them my own. I hope you will be blessed as you read them. I know you will find some that will become a permanent addition to your family. *(Please note: I received so many holiday traditions that it was decided to make them a separate book. If you sent me holiday traditions, be sure to look for them in the next book.)*

I noticed several distinct aspects of Adventist family traditions as I read your stories. Friday evening and Sabbath activities comprise your most important traditions. I received more traditions for these two occasions than for any others combined. You will notice this abundance reflected in the length of these chapters. Another important thing to you is staying in close touch with your family. Many of you make extraordinary efforts to connect with your family, be they close or far away.

If you don't have any traditions that mark you immediately as Adventist, don't worry. That's what this book is for. Not all of us were born into the Adventist Church and brought up with traditions passed down to us through our families. That's not a reason to become discouraged. It's a reason to get excited! We always have the opportunity to establish traditions in our own families that will possibly last until Jesus comes.

Every family and situation is different. In this book we will explore, not only Adventist family traditions, but also how we can customize those traditions for unique family situations. We can shape them to build for us a special history that will strengthen our bonds to family, church, and God. Allow me to be your hostess and introduce you to fellow believers around the world. Pull up a chair, brew a cup of tea, and let's visit.

CHAPTER ONE

Friday Evening

"What's so special about Sabbath?" my non-Adventist friends often ask me. One thing that makes Sabbath so special is Friday evening, because keeping Sabbath is about so much more than just attending a worship service at church. Sabbath is also about rest and celebration. It is time that's set aside to spend with family, friends, and God. I don't mow my lawn on Sabbath. I don't wash the car, work in my garden, or clean the house. The Sabbath hours are set aside. And the celebration begins on Friday evening.

Because so many people shared their traditions for Friday evening, I divided them up into two sections: Friday-evening celebrations and Friday-evening meals. I felt each deserved a chapter of its own.

Thankful Hearts

Although Friday-evening traditions contain many elements of celebration, family worship was one practice most consistently mentioned. Adventists are eager to worship God and thank Him for the blessing of the Sabbath, which begins on Friday evening at sundown.

"My husband and I have had this tradition since we were first married (thirty-one years ago). We sit in the living room, turn off the lights, and light candles. Then each of us tells what we are thankful for that happened during the previous week," says C. Jan Ogden. "My hubby even calls my mom and his mother every Friday evening, and they talk about what they are thankful for. We are 'empty-nesters,' and our children live all over the country—yet they call to tell us what they are thankful for on Friday evenings. (It's almost expected.)

"It's a simple thing, yet it has meant a lot to us as a family to praise God for His continual watch care and to be thankful for how He leads us throughout the week. God never gets tired of hearing our gratitude of what He does for us."

Music and Singing

Our worship often involves singing and musical talent. Pianos and guitars seem to be favorites. Gwen Simmons says, "Our family would always gather around on Friday evenings and sing. My mom or my sister would play the piano, my dad would play the guitar, my brother would sometimes play his banjo, and we'd all sing. Songs such as 'I Shall Not Be Moved,' 'Gloryland March,' and 'Camping in Canaan' still warm my heart. Even now, when we get together back home, we have our Friday-evening singing."

"In our home we always had evening worship," my friend Suzanne Perdew told me. "On Friday evenings we sang from the *Singing Youth* songbooks. As we kids got older, we would take turns playing the piano while the rest of the family sang."

Something about singing together draws people closer. I remember when we had newly converted friends who lived in our area. We would sit around in our living room, and I would play everything I knew from the *He Is Our Song* songbook on my guitar. If I couldn't play a song, we'd sing a cappella. It was wonderful to teach them our "old" favorites and learn new songs together. I still feel a warm glow remembering the good times we had.

"My family used to gather on Friday evenings after sundown and make music," wrote Ellen Ford of Greenbelt, Maryland. "My mother played the piano, my brother and my stepfather sang, and I would either play my flute or sing. It made Sabbath such a happy time. It was one of the few times when I felt that my family was close to each other. It wasn't necessarily a tradition, but someday, when I have a family of my own, I want to make it one."

Children love to sing. They enjoy it even better if they can accompany themselves with something loud and rhythmic. Rhythm instruments fit the bill, but don't let them get so loud you can't enjoy the singing anymore. This is difficult because children tend to become exuberant about playing. Limit younger children, who have trouble controlling the volume, to softer instruments, such as shakers and sandpaper blocks.

One of my ongoing projects is to increase our collection of rhythm instruments. I'll even add things that aren't strictly musical instruments. One time I found two old wooden bobbins at an antique store. They were inexpensive, so I bought them for the children to use as drumsticks or to hit together. Use your imagination. Your instruments do not need to be expensive or professional quality. A child will enjoy accompanying the song by rattling dried beans inside a small can just as much as having an expensive, carved maraca.

"Ever since my almost-twelve-year-old son was a tiny baby, we have sung the Sabbath song 'Who Am I?' to him," says Lisa Whitlow. "First we read the Bible lesson; then we have a story, songs, and prayer. Last we sing, 'I am someone special to Jesus . . . to Mommy . . . and to Daddy' to each of our three children. They are now twelve, nine, and six."

They may be small now, but children grow up quickly. And they take their memories with them. What you do today will influence their tomorrows. You may not realize it at this moment, but your are building the foundation for their future, one Sabbath at a time. It's impossible to tell what will influence them the most, which memory will be the one that stays with them the longest and be cherished the most.

For Marian Forschler it was a song from her school days. "When I was a student at Walla Walla College, on Friday evenings the deans always had us sing 'Now the Day Is Over.' It was also played softly while we came and went from a rather hushed worship at the beginning of the Sabbath. These college memories happened more than thirty-five years ago. About twenty years ago I met someone who'd also attended WWC, and this song had meant much to her also. Everyone in her congregation knew that she loved this song. When she and her family left for a mission assignment, the church family gave them a recording containing this and other quiet, restful songs."

No matter what their ages, take care not to underestimate your children's abilities. They thrive on participation, and it prepares them for taking their place in the church family. Encourage them to do as much as they are able in your worship services. Sandra Cruz's children carried the family worship. "In Friday worship the children chose and read the scripture. They told the Sabbath School lesson—at that time it was the same lesson for both primary and juniors. They prayed. We adults just listened. They even preached occasionally when the weather was too bad to go out."

We will focus on special food in the chapter on Friday-evening meals, but it is worth mentioning that Friday-evening and Saturday-evening activities accompanied by special treats will be that much more memorable. My husband kids me because I still remember what snack my mother made every time our family went to the drive-in theater when I was a child. (Remember, I told you in the Introduction that I became a Seventh-day Adventist when I was nineteen.) And just the mention of certain annual television specials brings back fond memories of Rice Krispies® treats (with chocolate chips!). Looking forward to special treats was something that kept Katherine Neff returning to her neighbors' family night. It could be something that keeps our own or our neighborhood children looking forward to *our* worships.

"When I was a child, I grew up in a neighborhood filled with children," remembers Katherine. "My mother was a member of our local Adventist church, but my father was not a Christian—which made it difficult to have regular sundown worship as a family. Occasionally, my mother allowed my three sisters and me to share 'family night' with our Latter-day Saints neighbors on Wednesday evenings. I really enjoyed singing silly songs with their five children and was impressed that their daddy was there to sing and read to them.

"I have to admit, my favorite time of the evening was treat time at the close. There were always homemade doughnuts, popcorn balls, or brownies for everyone! I've grown up and have children of my own, and I want to recreate that 'family time' in my home. It isn't easy now with two teenage boys, especially when half our family of four 'doesn't sing'! But we still get together on Friday evening after dinner is cleared away. Currently we are reading the stories from *Patriarchs and Prophets,* and I try to remember to make treats. They are just as popular with teenage boys as they were with little girls!

"My oldest son likes to pick up Bible or inspirational nature videos from the local library, which we enjoy watching while we're munching our treats. The time we share together to hear about God's plan for us and His great love means so much to me. I hope it will bless my children as well and will be a tradition that they will want to carry on if they marry and have families of their own."

Any time adults devote their undivided attention to children, they are bound to make a lasting impression. When they do it with a little creativity, it makes a great impression. It doesn't take much—just something the children anticipate each week, knowing they can count on it. Like being swung into the air.

"Because of my husband Helmuth's German heritage," Sue Fritz told me, "we decided to continue a family tradition he had as a child to welcome and close the Sabbath. At the end of the prayer, which was done in a circle kneeling, they all stood, joined hands, and said in German, 'God's blessing on the Sabbath day.' Then the children were swung into the air by those holding their hands while they all remained in the circle. This was the part he especially loved, as did our two girls.

"As Sabbath concluded with a worship and prayer, the ritual was repeated, but with the change to the German for 'God's blessing in the new week.' We still do this ritual as the 'kids' are home with friends, and we hope to continue if we are blessed with grandchildren. It always seemed to light up the children's eyes and add even more joy to a time with Jesus."

Candles

Candles play a large part in our evening worship services. We have different traditions for lighting them, but they are lighted for the same basic reasons.

(A cautionary note about candles: Never leave them unattended. Place candles where they will not reach anything flammable. And above all, do not leave children alone with lighted candles for even a second. Children are dangerously attracted to fire. Be sure also to store matches well out of their reach.) Any candle, be it store-bought or homemade, will fit the bill. Some are a bit more traditional, perhaps, than others, but choice is largely dictated by personal preference. Small white Hanukkah candles can be purchased inexpensively in the grocery store, as can birthday candles. Beeswax candles have a pleasant smell and don't drip. We use gold candles in our candelabra. If you are using candles at the dinner table, make sure they are unscented so they will not compete with the aromas of the food.

"When we were young," Jeff Scoggins told me, "we would start the Sabbath by gathering around the coffee table (or similar piece of furniture low enough for kids to reach), and we would each light our own little candle. Then we said the fourth commandment together. After that we sat there in the living room and ate popcorn and fruit as a family and talked all evening. We still eat popcorn and fruit when I visit my parents on a Friday evening."

Dixie Plata says, "Every Friday evening we light candles, one for each of us, and place them on the table. We enjoy eating our meal by candlelight. This atmosphere helps us slow down from our busy day and remember the Sabbath. We almost always have stew or soup and homemade bread. The good smells mean Sabbath is here."

One of the things we are eager to do on Friday evening is to thank God for bringing us safely through another week. We thank Him for the blessings He has given us. And we thank Him for the rest we are about to enjoy. Some of us have found unique ways to thank Him.

"One thing we've done that I love is light a tiny (cut short) birthday candle and sit in silence while the sun is going down," Elizabeth Howe told me. "During this time we are thinking about the week before. After the candle goes out, my husband, Ted, says a prayer, and then we share specific kind things other people have done for us during the past week or things we have done for others. I'm not great about praising spontaneously, but when I know I'm going to have this 'opportunity,' it helps me come up with all kinds of happenings to share.

"Especially when our children were younger, it was a wonderful chance to praise them for little specific kindnesses we caught them doing, and it was a benefit to do it in front of the whole family or any guests we had (guests were urged to participate). We also encouraged them to talk about what they had done for someone else.

"Now, I save thank-you cards we've received in the mail (or email) to read to everyone. I watch for other visual aides—for example, if I was stuck somewhere and someone loaned me money to make a phone call, I can bring money to worship and ask the others to guess what happened. If I gave someone a loaf of bread, I could bring a loaf of bread. The visuals would be good to use with younger children. Jumper cables—now what do you think I brought those to worship for?"

We so seldom pause and take time to thank others for what they have done for us. This tradition would help us to become more aware of the blessings God gives us by encouraging us to note them during the week. You might keep a notebook somewhere central, perhaps in the kitchen, where you can jot down specifics that would be lost to a fickle memory. Or you might try decorating a box and cutting a slit in the top to drop in pieces of paper with notes about what happened. Be sure to keep a pad of paper and a pen handy (or better yet attached) to the box so no one has an excuse for not writing a note when something wonderful happens.

Some busy families have a central whiteboard where they leave notes for each other and keep each other apprised of schedule changes. One area of the whiteboard could be reserved for recording blessings. In addition to being convenient, it would afford a daily testimonial about God's work for all to see.

I recently heard someone talk about how little we notice God's goodness anymore. Like the people of Jesus' day, we cry for miracles when they occur every day in front of our noses. Isn't feeding one as difficult as feeding four thousand? Every day that we have three meals on our table we should be incredibly grateful. We have been fed! A good share of the world goes hungry. Every bite is a miracle. By nurturing this attitude of gratitude, we will begin to find many things to be thankful for in our everyday lives that we never even saw before.

Bodil Morris has a tradition called the "Thankfuls." After lighting the "Sabbath Candle" during Friday-evening worship, each person would have a time to share something he or she was thankful for that week. "We start with the youngest and go to the oldest, so if we had visitors, we would be able to have an order based on our tradition," she says. "No matter who would visit, Daddy was always the oldest and would conclude the time of 'Thankfuls' to God. After a time of 'Thankfuls,' we would end with prayer."

I personally like the idea of candles because even if you don't use them as your only light source on Friday evening, they contribute to the sense of peace and worship we are creating. Candlelight is tranquil. It's hard to be "busy" around candles. Our internal springs start to unwind. The flicker of candlelight is like hearing the surf or smelling balsam or petting a dog. It begins that journey into relaxation and rest.

"In our own home we have a large pillar candle with three wicks," says Faith Laughlin. "We call it our Sabbath candle. We light it at sundown worship on Friday. The last one to bed blows it out for the night. We try to light it again after returning from church so we can have it burning until sundown worship on Sabbath. Sometimes that means we re-light it just before Sabbath vespers and blow it out at the end of the devotional.

"This tradition started years ago when I would visit

my grandmother's house. The two of us were the only Adventists in the family, so I often spent Friday night and Sabbath with her. We would put on some Sabbath music, light a candle, and sing along. Sometimes we would read by a small lamp while looking up every now and then to see the candle flickering on the shelf."

> *"On Friday evening we light the Sabbath candle (a Hanukkah candle found in the Jewish section of the grocery store). It stays lighted for twenty-four hours."* —Pixie Paradis

Once at a retreat, a woman asked me if we should use candles. I think she was referring to their association with the New Age movement, making them unsuitable for "sacred" use. If you have similar concerns, maybe candles aren't for you. They certainly aren't mandatory. But I think they can add a beautiful element to our worship. As with everything, your motive is what matters most. Unless you are using candles specifically made to balance your chakras and are hoping for that effect, I don't see a problem with them. In the end, you are the one who can best determine if candles should be added to your worship.

Sabbath Surprise

Boy, oh boy, does this one get the blue ribbon. When the emails began pouring in with all the family tradition suggestions, even my husband couldn't help but get interested. He read most of them, but this one really impressed him. The first Sabbath after we received it, he had not only purchased the Sabbath surprise himself, but had hidden it and was, if possible, even more anxious than the children were for them to find it. Our children are young, which could account for it, but they take great pleasure in the Sabbath surprise. It's now something they look forward to each week.

I don't know who gets the credit for creating it, but several versions of "Sabbath surprises" came in. Gwen Simmons told me, "This tradition started when I was a kid. Mom would always buy some kind of treat for Sabbath dinner and call it a 'Sabbath surprise.' I'm sure there were a variety of treats, but the only one I remember is giant frosted animal crackers. We continued this tradition with my own children, except we used the Sabbath surprise for Friday evenings. At sunset, we would hide the treat, and the kids would have to find it."

For small children, hiding it in easy, obvious places is a good idea. But, for older children, you can do really elaborate treasure hunts or leave a paper trail of clues. Our son Joshua is just starting to read, so a set of simply worded clues would be more exciting for him than just looking around for a hiding spot. And the game would also reinforce his reading skills.

"When the boys were little, we would have a Sabbath surprise that we would hide somewhere in the room," wrote Bodil Morris. "The boys would look forward to seeking and finding the surprise during Friday-evening worship. The surprise could range from a little edible treat to some little Sabbath toy or stickers. Now that the boys are older, we have a special Sabbath drink, non-alcoholic grape juice. We have Sabbath goblets that we use. This reminds us that Jesus told us to remember Him when we drink the cup."

"One simple thing that our three-year-old

daughter loves is bath bubbles. We put bubbles in the bathtub only on Friday evening. Blowing bubbles is another favorite for her. She has special bath toys for Sabbath also. She asks almost every night if it is Sabbath yet so that we can have bubbles and sing." –DAVID AND KATHY IWASA

Material items aren't the only things you can include in your Sabbath surprises. Barbara Zaremsky has been doing Sabbath surprises with her nine-year-old daughter for five years. "Sometimes it would be something as simple as a pencil or ruler with her name on it, sometimes a bigger gift, like a computer game. It all depended on what we had on hand and what was going on at the time. Now that she's older, it is getting a little harder to find simple weekly gifts for her, so we've recently changed the program.

"We now have a basket with slips of paper containing special privileges for the week. Examples are two uninterrupted hours with Dad (he's a minister, so this is a real special one), staying up a half hour later one night during the week, no chores for one day, eating out at a favorite restaurant. Our daughter has never gotten tired of her Sabbath surprises. I believe this has helped to make Sabbath really special for her."

IDEAS FOR SABBATH SURPRISES

Stickers *Watercolor paints*
Modeling clay *Specialty crayons*
Candy *Sabbath video*
Doodle pads *Gum*
Markers *Bubble bath*
Stamps *Bubbles for blowing*
Sabbath cassette tapes *Balloons*

Games

For me it is reassuring to have things that are reserved for Sabbath use, even though I do not believe that our lives should be divided up into "sacred" and "secular." Far too often we compartmentalize the sacred. We should not be worldly during the week and holy on the Sabbath. In order for us to be effective Christians and have a growing, meaningful, vital relationship with God, every day we must allow Him access to all parts of our lives. But, there are certain things that, when saved specifically for Sabbath, mean more because they are not used commonly. Children can have special toys; adults might have a certain activity, for example, a hobby like painting. Certain games, too, can be set aside for Sabbath.

"I always kept special toys, books, and games (appropriate for Sabbath) for my kids when they were small for Friday night and Sabbath," says Marian Forschler. "I kept them in plastic dishpans up on a high shelf. It was always a time of excitement when we got them down on Friday evening."

In New Zealand, solo mum Judi Larsen says their favorite family time together is when the kids all crawl into her bed and they read a mission story together. "The kids sometimes color or draw pictures while they listen," she says, "We usually do this on a Friday evening, but it's fine for any time. On Sabbath we play nature or Bible games. Sometimes we go for a bike ride out into the country or to the park."

Games—those interactive, family-friendly amusements—went out of vogue when TV and video games came onto the scene. If you ask me, that's where the family started to unravel. The family that played together, stopped eating meals together, found solitary amusements, and hasn't been the same since. Ideally, Friday evenings or Saturday nights are not the only times your family gets together to play. But, if they are, make the most of them. Think of it this way, when you are old and gray and looking back over your life, you will never, ever say, "Didn't we have a great time watching that television program? Wasn't that fun?" But, you will remember the fun of playing together.

"Every Friday evening Mother read to us. While she read, the four of us (with a twelve-year age range) would put together 'Sabbath' jigsaw puzzles (Jesus knocking at the door, scenery, an angel protecting two children on a bridge). We were listening but still involved in doing an activity." —DIXIE PLATA

"We did the typical Friday-evening worship with songs, stories, Bible Tic Tac Toe, and charades," recalls Joan Hutchinson. "Our favorite activity was Puzzle Race. Each family member would select one of several 100-piece nature puzzles. Then all five of us would squeeze our pieces onto the dining-room table, prepare the pieces photo up (no pieces interlocking). When everyone was ready, we'd race to see who would finish first.

"It was such fun, especially when the capable, well-educated, brilliant father always came in last. My husband and I learned that children need to see that they can be 'best' at something. Though the children are grown and have moved away, the game lives on. We just introduced a young friend to Puzzle Race last Saturday night. He won, of course, and Dad came in last again."

ADVENTIST FAMILY TRADITIONS • 23

> *"My wife Martha and I have a Sabbath tradition: We spend Friday evening and Sabbath afternoon putting together picture puzzles while listening to sacred music."* –Thurman C. Petty, Jr.

Miscellaneous

Sometimes our traditions begin spontaneously with no conscious decision to begin a tradition. It just develops. That's what happened to Gerald and Sybil du Preez of Somerset West, South Africa. "Around 1984 I had had a particularly stressful week," says Gerald. "When I arrived home that Friday afternoon, my wife had set the table, complete with special 'champagne' glasses containing red grape juice. She had covered the box in which our steam iron had been packaged with brightly colored wrapping paper. In the box she had placed some chocolate bars, one for each member of the family.

"We welcomed the Sabbath by wishing each other a happy Sabbath and clinking our glasses. After supper, each one had to reach into the box and select a chocolate bar without looking inside. Our daughters, ages five and three at that time, were excited about this little 'ceremony.' Some Friday evenings after that, I would have to hide the chocolates (after the girls had selected them from the box), and they would go on a treasure hunt to find their chocolates.

"Today, our daughters are twenty-one, nineteen, and fourteen. Friday evenings are not Friday evenings without the grape juice and chocolate bars (although I don't hide them anymore!). Any guests in our home are included in this little ritual. What was originally intended by my wife as something to give my spirits a lift after a tough week has become a fond family tradition that all of us look forward to."

For Trudy Wright, mission stories have become a tradition. "Friday nights the kids settled in bed with me, and we read mission stories," she says.

Think about your own family life for a minute. What little quirky things does your family do that have potential for becoming a tradition? When I asked people to share their traditions, some wrote, "We have nothing special. We just do things we have always done." But, really, what is a tradition? It is something that holds meaning for your family. Let me give you an example. My grandfather, now passed away, was Italian. We celebrated Christmas with my grandparents on Christmas Eve because "the Italians did it that way." Grandpa handed out Torrone®, an Italian nougat candy. It was the only time of year we ate them.

After my grandfather passed away, my dad bought a box of Torrones, and the first Christmas we celebrated without Grandpa, Dad passed them out. It hit me then that this was a tradition. It held meaning for us. Even though it was "just something we had always done," it held significance. If it hadn't, my Dad wouldn't have continued the practice. Your traditions are the things that your family does. Maybe no one else does it. Maybe no one else would consider it a tradition. But for your family, it has significance. It is your tradition. Celebrate, preserve, and cherish the things that make your family special.

"We have a tradition we began when the kids were very small and wanted to sleep with us," Jeannie Fehl told me. "Since I did enjoy it occasionally, my husband and I decided it would be a Friday-night treat. They slept with me every Friday evening for several years when they were little. That made Sabbath coming even more exciting for them. They couldn't wait for Friday night. My husband didn't mind sleeping alone once a week because I talk in my sleep, so it was a joy for him to be in another room and get an uninterrupted night's sleep."

> *"When I was a kid, we always said the Lord's Prayer in unison at the end of the blessing—we took turns saying the blessing too. This was always an important part of beginning Sabbath."*
> –MARIAN FORSCHLER

JEWISH ROOTS

More than one person wrote to tell me of traditions they had that have Jewish roots. I have a strong interest in this area myself and was intrigued by these traditions. Some traditions were more elaborate than others.

"We try to sing as a family the Jewish song 'Now the Sabbath Queen weds the people of God' every night and light a candle," wrote David and Kathy Iwasa. "It began after working at Thunderbird Adventist Academy in Arizona, where Pastor Don Pate would sing it at vespers to begin the Sabbath. Now that we have two children, we light two candles—one for each of them to blow out (equality in all, you know)."

Many times we can adapt Jewish traditions and customs to fit our own families. The Blackwelders did this. "Our family is interested in Jewish traditions that have to do with the Sabbath," Lois Blackwelder, campus chaplain at Walla Walla College, told me. "We were in a Jewish bookstore several years ago when we purchased a menorah. We used it each Friday evening when our children were small in a way I am sure that it is never used in a Jewish home, but we enjoyed it.

"The menorah was on the dinner table each Friday evening. Before we began our meal, either my husband Tim or I would begin to light the candles; and our children, Glenn and Holly, would say a day of the week. We left the top candle for last, and as we were lighting it, we would ask the question 'Which day is the best of all?' The children would answer 'Sabbath!' and we would light the last candle on the top."

As you can see, borrowing from Jewish traditions can be creative and doesn't necessarily follow any strict guidelines. If you should want to stick a little closer to the original tradition, you can do that too. Ed Christian, editor of the *Journal of the Adventist Theological Society,* sent me one of the most fascinating traditions involving Jewish roots.

"In my family," he said, "the most interesting 'traditions' occur on Friday evening as we welcome in the Sabbath. They are just for fun, but we've been doing them for quite a few years, and if we forget part of it, the children remind us.

"For Friday night supper there is always homemade soup and bread. We eat by candlelight. Before we eat, we each, one at a time, sing the Hebrew blessing on the bread, just as Jesus and His disciples would have at the Last Supper, then say it in English: *'Baruch atah Adonai, Elohenu, Melek ha olam, ha motzi lechem min ha'aretz'* ('Blessed art Thou, O Lord, God, King of eternity, who brings forth bread from the earth'). After each person sings, he or she tears off a piece of the slice of bread being passed around the table and eats it.

"There is also a goblet of grape juice on the table. We next pass that around and each take a sip. Before we do, though, we once again sing in Hebrew and then translate, this time the blessing Jesus would have pronounced on the wine at the Last Supper: *'Baruch atah Adonai, Eloheynu, Melek ha'olam, bouray peri ha'gafen'* ('Blessed art Thou, O Lord, God, King of eternity, who creates the fruit of the vine').

"Then I pray, *'Baruch atah Adonai, Elohenu, Melek ha olam, Melek ha shabbat, Melek ha shabbat shalom, amen'* ('Blessed art Thou, O Lord, God, King of eternity, King of the Sabbath, King of Sabbath peace'), but I don't translate it. Everyone responds by wishing each other 'Shabbat shalom!'

"After the meal, we sing Psalm 133 as a round, as we learned it from Richard Davidson, Chair of the Old Testament Department at the seminary at Andrews. We maintain the rhythm by pounding our fists on the table on the first beat of every measure. We begin slowly, then double the speed. The singing is vigorous and stirs our blood.

"The last part of the supper is blowing out the candles. We take turns blowing them out. Each person, before blowing, has to share something for which he or she is thankful. These little traditions help separate the Sabbath from the weekday world. We all look forward to something that happens once every week, and so is expected, and yet is different from all other nights of the week. By the time we have finished these traditions, we are quiet and calm; we have entered into Shabbat Shalom."

This transliteration is merely phonetic and bears little relation to the actual transliteration of the words in such a way that a Hebrew speaker would recognize them.

PSALM 133

How good and pleasant it is when brothers live together in unity [lit. "festal oneness"]! It is like precious oil poured on the head, running down on the beard, running down on Aaron's beard, down upon the collar of his robes. It is as if the dew of [Mount] Hermon were falling on Mount Zion. For there the LORD bestows his blessing, even life forevermore. [Note the climactic parallelism in the middle of this psalm.]

The song on page 30 in Hebrew is considered one of the oldest extant Hebrew psalm tunes. Perhaps unchanged since the time of Christ. It is a "song of ascents" sung by pilgrims climbing Mount Zion to worship at the temple during the festivals. The song consists of the first verse of the psalm. [Note that the "ch" sound is gutteral, like clearing the throat.]

As I learned, we have many ways to welcome the Sabbath. Our Friday evenings are special times of family and tradition. They are times of thankfulness and peace. Together we welcome the Lord of the Sabbath into our hearts and our homes.

Henay Ma Tov*

*Music transcribed by Mary Christian

Chapter Two

The Friday-Evening Meal

One of the most universal Adventist traditions is the special Friday-evening meal. The food itself varies from family to family, many of the customs and foods tying families to their ethnic roots—and, occasionally, to someone else's ethnic roots. My friends, the Edisons, often have palachinkas for their Friday-evening meal. Palachinkas are thin pancakes filled with a variety of stuffings—Nutella®, peanut butter, jelly, cottage cheese, sour cream and jelly (or anything else you want). The tradition of serving this German dish did not begin because either Rich or Ana have German ancestry. Rich is Scotch-Irish, Dutch, Welsh, English, French, and German. Ana is Puerto Rican. But Ana grew up with the Satelmajer family. Elder Nikolaus Satelmajer is a German from Yugoslavia, and that is how their tradition began.

Ethnic food happens to be my favorite kind. I don't care what type it is. I'll try anything: Thai,

Korean, Mexican, Indian, Italian, Spanish, Chinese, French, Hungarian, Cajun, German. I'm not sure if it's the diversity I like or the fact that most ethnic food I've tried is pretty spicy. My friends Rachel and Gary Kinne prepared the same Italian meal each Friday night for a number of years. "When Gary and I married, we wanted to make Friday evening special, so we chose a favorite meal (spaghetti, garlic bread, and veggies) every Friday night," Rachel said. "After three or four years, our children asked if we could change the Friday-evening meal. We chose to alternate between tacos and spaghetti. As time has passed, we have stopped alternating and have tacos every Friday evening. It has become our welcome meal to

RACHEL KINNE'S TACOS

1 20-ounce can Worthington® *Vegetarian Burger*®
1 medium potato, peeled and shredded
1/2 packet Lawry's® taco seasoning
1/2 head iceberg lettuce, shredded
1 pound mild cheddar cheese, shredded
2 packages taco shells (total of 24 shells)
Picante or taco sauce

Place burger and shredded potato in frying pan with oil. Sprinkle with taco seasoning. Cook until well-browned, turning occasionally.

Place shells on cookie sheet so they stand upright. (Place one upside down over the top of two for stabilization.) When the burger is nearly done, place taco shells in 350°F oven for 7 to 10 minutes. Remove shells from oven, fill with burger mixture, lettuce, and cheese; top with sauce. Serve immediately.

the Sabbath."

Ken Caviness, who teaches in the physics department of Southern Adventist University, grew up to a Friday-evening meal of lentil soup and Danish Dessert®, which is similar to fruit-flavored pudding.

"People often put fruit in it," Ken says, "making a sort of soft Jell-O®. It's brought to a boil and then cooled, like a pudding. When I was a kid, I used to beg my mom for a taste while it was still hot! Now in my own family, we blend two sets of traditions, so we don't do this every week; but usually once every two or three weeks we still make lentil soup."

Esther Caviness's Lentil Soup

1 16-ounce package of dried lentils (picked over and rinsed thoroughly)
Chopped onion (or dried onion flakes) to taste
Minced fresh garlic (or garlic powder) to taste
Salt to taste
1 10 3/4-ounce can condensed tomato soup
1 cup milk (can substitute evaporated or soy milk)
Crackers (optional)
Emmentaler Swiss cheese, cubed (optional)

Combine lentils and seasonings in pressure cooker; cook under pressure for 20 minutes. Add tomato soup and milk; cook without pressure until hot. Serve immediately.

SERVING SUGGESTION: Offer crackers or small cubes of Swiss cheese as garnish.

"Hundreds of different kinds of cheese are made in Switzerland," says Ken. "During the time we spent in Europe, we found out that if we asked for 'Swiss cheese,' people would say, 'Yes, but what kind of Swiss cheese?'"

If you can't find Emmentaler, Ken suggests using another type of Swiss. (You could try Gruyere. Or since he says that seeing it get stringy when you dipped out a spoonful of soup was half the fun, maybe a combination of mozzarella and mild cheddar.) "Nowadays we try to go light on cheese and other dairy products, but cutting up tiny bits of Swiss cheese in my Friday-supper lentil soup is a strong memory from my childhood!"

My friend Sharon Buttrick told me about a tradition her family borrowed from their good friends, the Trecartins, in Michigan. "We make braided challah bread for our evening meal (usually a homemade soup). We light candles and then for the prayer we sing 'Bless Our Home.' It's sung to the tune of 'Edelweiss.'

Bless our home, bless our food;
Come, O Lord, and sit with us;
May our talk glow with peace,
May Your love surround us;
Friendship and love, may they bloom and grow,
Bloom and grow forever;
Bless our home, bless our food;
Come, O Lord, and sit with us. [1]

We join hands to sing the prayer. I have copies of the words to give guests so that they can join us in prayer."

Meals don't have to be elaborate to be remembered. "Our family always enjoyed a bowl of rice and bran muffins come Friday night," says Christie Hodson of Oxford, Maine. "Often, if we'd beg, our parents would light a few candles, and we'd eat in the dim light. There was always something comforting about the familiarity of that tradition."

The food might not even have as much to do with the tradition as how it's eaten. Our family doesn't have a particular Friday-evening meal, but we generally eat it in the same way each week. The table is set with a formal French setting as if we were expecting company, which we usually are not on Friday evening. I try to have fresh flowers on the table, either in a vase or blooming in a pot, depending on the season.

We light a candelabrum with three gold candles. After the lighting of the candles and a special blessing, the children search for their Sabbath surprises. The actual courses are fairly elaborate, but not much different from what you would find at our table any other day of the week because I enjoy cooking for my family. The biggest difference is that we have dessert. It's the only night of the week I make dessert, so that's a treat.

Really, though, the meal isn't only about the food; it's about family and companionship, sharing, and socializing. "During the years our kids were growing up," Dick Duerksen wrote me, "Friday evenings always included a special meal—either cornbread and chili or Scotch oat cakes and fruit soup. After the meal, there was a story and prayer and long conversation about life. It was the best day of the week." *What* you eat doesn't matter so much as *how* you eat it and with whom.

Linda Downs's family starts Sabbath with a traditional Friday-evening meal of *Schnitze Supp* (a Volga

German version of fruit soup, consisting of hot thickened fruit over toast). "We have a special family worship, which includes singing with piano, guitars, bass guitar, or violin. Then someone reads aloud from the *Adventist Review* or a religious book. We end with a special Sabbath prayer."

Sometimes it's a combination of food that brings back strong memories of Friday-evening suppers. For Diane Pearson, Dean of Women at Walla Walla College, it was the pairing of Nuteena® sandwiches and pea soup. "My parents became vegetarians when I was about ten years old (in the 1950s)," recalls Diane. "Our Friday-evening supper became a tradition of Nuteena® sandwiches and green-pea soup. To this day I still get a warm, cozy feeling when I eat either or both of the items that represented a special part of our family tradition."

My friend, Pat Moore, had a wonderful surprise one Friday evening. Her husband volunteered to cook supper. Little did she realize at the time that his entrée would become a tradition in their home. "Fridays always seem to have more chores—cleaning, cooking, laundry—than hours," Pat says. "And if you want to share a Sabbath meal with some friends after church, well, that just adds a bit more work. I was delighted when PJ offered to cook dinner!

"We had been married for less than a year at the time and found ourselves clear across the continent, far from family and friends. PJ was in medical school, and I was a nurse working at the Medical Center. I was a bit skeptical when I asked him what we were having and he told me I'd have to wait and see.

"It was worth the wait. On the table he had applesauce, peanut butter, butter, and syrup, and a freshly baked homemade waffle."

The Friday-evening waffle tradition lived on to delight even the friends of their now-grown children. Pat says they still encounter the response, "Waffles? For supper?" when guests, invited for supper, find "breakfast" on the table. If you want to surprise your friends, try their recipe.

Pat and P.J. Moore's Waffles

3/4 cup oil
3 cups flour
5 1/4 teaspoons baking powder
3/4 teaspoons salt
2 tablespoons sugar

1/2 cup buttermilk powder
4 eggs, separated
2 1/4 to 2 1/2 cups water
1 1/2 teaspoons vanilla

In a large bowl, combine flour, baking powder, salt, sugar, and buttermilk powder. Set aside.

In a medium bowl, beat egg whites until very stiff and dry. (You can't get them too stiff!)

Add egg yolks to water; mix. Add to dry ingredients. Add oil; mix well. Last, add the vanilla. Fold in egg whites. *(You may need to add more water to the batter to reach the right consistency for baking.)* Cook according to waffle iron's directions. *Try sprinkling chopped pecans on top the waffle before closing the waffle iron. Delicious!*

"Let yourself be creative with the variety of toppings," Pat urges. "Thicken some fresh or frozen blueberries. Any fresh fruit topped with whipped cream or a nondairy whip is delicious! Try mushroom sauce for a savory variation. Honey is a favorite as well."

The simple act of eating while surrounded by the warmth and security of our families can often endow many otherwise plain foods with exquisite flavor. "The main tradition I recall from my childhood home focuses on food," says Cecille Hansen. "Friday-evening suppers, to be exact. In summer, my mother, Muriel Thompson, made her incredible potato salad (see p. 59). We'd have that with cold Heinz® baked beans and bread and butter.

"She made this a couple of years ago when my brother came to visit—a rare time all of us adult kids were together—and it brought such good feelings. In winter, we had two Friday-evening menus: her homemade potato soup or cornbread, applesauce, and milk gravy. The latter is still a "delicacy" in our home. I don't know what magic Mom uses to make milk, flour, margarine, and salt taste so good."

Muriel Thompson's Friday-Evening Potato Soup

"This recipe is great for surprise company," says Muriel. "Just add more potatoes, etc. until you have enough."

5 medium white potatoes, peeled and cubed
1/2 medium onion, sliced

1 12-ounce can evaporated milk
1/2 teaspoon salt

Place potatoes and onion in a large pan. Add salt; cover with water. Cook until potatoes are soft. *Try to have some cooking water left in pan.* Mash with potato masher until smooth, then add evaporated milk *(Muriel uses Pet® brand).* Mix well. *If the soup is too thick, add regular milk until it reaches the desired consistency. Serves about four.*

*Author's note: This recipe is very similar to one I make. For my variation add vegetable bouillon to the cooking water and include two diced carrots with the potatoes. The cooked carrot gives the soup a really pretty color. If you don't want to use milk, skip it. The taste is nearly as good. Or put a 16-ounce block of tofu in the blender and add to the soup in place of the milk. The consistency is different, but the taste is great. To prepare this soup for Sabbath, you can cook the potatoes and carrots ahead and warm them before mashing and adding remaining ingredients. This soup goes great with my recipe for cheese biscuits.

CÉLESTE'S MAY-I-HAVE-THE-RECIPE? CHEESE BISCUITS

1 1/2 cups all-purpose flour
1 1/2 teaspoons baking powder
1/2 teaspoon salt
4 tablespoons (1/2 cube) cold unsalted butter or margarine

1 egg
1/2 cup milk
1 cup shredded sharp cheddar cheese
1/4 cup shredded Parmesan cheese

Preheat oven to 400°F. Mix first three ingredients in a large bowl. Add butter, blending in with your fingers or a pastry blender until it resembles fine granules. Add egg and milk. Blend with a fork until it forms a soft ball.

Turn out onto a floured surface; pat down to about the thickness of pita bread. Sprinkle cheeses on top. Knead 10 to 20 times to incorporate the cheese. Pat down again to a generous thickness. *The trick with these is not to make them flat as pancakes. It won't seem like you'll get many biscuits, but they will be like little skyscrapers. One batch is enough for a family of four. If your family is larger or you are having guests, plan to make more. They disappear fast.* Cut with your favorite biscuit cutter. Repeat this process with any remaining scraps of dough.

Place the biscuits on ungreased cookie sheet and bake for 10 to 13 minutes. Remove from oven when biscuits begin to brown. Cool on a wire rack.

In many ways our climates dictate what our comfort foods are. During frosty weather, we favor hot, savory soups and entrees that will warm us from the inside out. During warm weather, it's a different matter. Kathy Phillips, who grew up in the tropics, wouldn't think much of my soups. (But, I envy her mother the backrubs.) "As a child living in the tropics," Kathy told me, "we had cold fruit soup and cinnamon rolls for Friday-evening supper. Then our family of four would lounge on my parents' king-size bed in the air-conditioned bedroom, and Mom would read stories to us while we rubbed her back and legs."

"My mother, Beth Coffin, has a very simple recipe for cold fruit soup. Boil a quantity of tapioca until done. Cool and add a can of frozen concentrate grape juice. Cut up and add fruit of your choice as for a fruit salad." —KATHY PHILLIPS

Some of our favorite foods come to us from our school experiences. Adventists must have invented haystacks (a variation of taco salad made of piles of corn chips, lettuce, beans, tomatoes, cheese, black olives, and salsa). We devoured piles of them on a school trip to Camp Lauroweld after we had conquered Tumbledown Mountain. Corndogs always make me think of the International Festival we had at Pine Tree Academy the year I attended. Sharon Kamp worked in the cafeteria of the boarding school she attended and recalls special foods they prepared for Sabbath.

"I remember that Friday at home and at boarding school we worked hard to prepare foods for the Sabbath. At school we always made cinnamon rolls topped with maple glaze and cashews. At home I helped wash the wheat flour to form gluten and make lentil loaves or patties."

Food, in its various forms, nourishes our bodies. But the companionship we enjoy around our Sabbath table nourishes our souls. God, in His goodness, has given us both healthful, delicious food and wonderful people to share it with. With Him at the head of the table, your Sabbath will truly be blessed.

---

1. *Celebrate the Feasts* by Martha Zimmerman. Minneapolis: Bethany House Publishers, 1981.

Chapter Three

Sabbath Worship, Service, and Rest

It's an age-old question in Adventism. What to do on Sabbath? Though the Bible gives basic guidelines, there are probably as many answers to that question as there are cultures represented in our denomination. Worship, music, enjoying nature, and socializing (both with each other and in witnessing endeavors) seem to be the most popular. Since witnessing is not confined to Sabbath, we'll talk about it more in a separate chapter (see chapter 8: "Witnessing").

When I was growing up, my family was what I would consider musical. We never played in the symphony, but we regularly burst into song to pass the time on car trips or while working together. It was not at all unusual to fall asleep to the sound of my mother singing as she went about her work. She had a beautiful voice, and complete strangers would compliment her on it between hymns at church. After we began attending the Adventist Church, we were frequently asked to perform special music.

Sharing music bonds people together. The music you listen to or produce reflects your heart. Do we sing when we are upset or angry? It's very hard. Singing and playing music is a joyful sharing of ourselves with others. When this is done as an act of worship, it is very powerful.

"When I was a child we always visited grandparents on Sabbath afternoon," recalls Lesley McGrath. "It was fun to catch up with all the cousins. Sabbath was (and in some ways still is) a family day. As we cousins have formed our own families, it is a lot harder to accomplish. Another thing we did was gather around the piano or organ and sing to our hearts' content. Some in our family are beautiful singers."

The fun of singing or playing instruments in a group is hard to beat. Even though my talent with musical instruments is negligible, I still get excited about jamming with other musicians. It has its moments, but when everything comes together, the result is something you don't easily forget.

"A tradition that my family had while I was growing up was playing musical instruments together on Sabbath," says Peggy Harris. "Either Friday evening or Sabbath afternoon, my dad would play his cello, my brother his violin, and me, the piano. This was sometimes a painful experience because the music didn't come together much.

"My dad played by ear and would stumble along a few paces behind my brother and me. I thought this was a pain in the neck at the time. But looking back in later years, I realized that this was one of the few things we ever did together and have to come to relish that precious memory of stumbling through music—together."

Besides being a great family day, Sabbath is a time to spend with friends and relatives we might not otherwise get a chance to visit with during the week. "A tradition we had," Kimberly Harris told me, "was to spend the entire Sabbath with close friends—from sundown to sundown, except for the time we were sleeping. We spent Friday evening with our good friends Ron and Deria Gadsden, and then after church on Sabbath we ate a potluck dinner with a few other families and spent the afternoon together. Finally we had Saturday-evening vespers at the church. Although we didn't have company every week, we did it often enough that it seems that way."

A Sabbath afternoon walk has to be one of the most popular Sabbath activities. There are a few favorite spots we visit over and over. Sometimes we take the canoe out and spend the afternoon in a secluded spot where we can tie up and be by ourselves. Occasionally a group from church will organize a hike on the Long Trail (a trail that runs the length of Vermont) or in the Adirondack Mountains in nearby New York. Wherever we go, it's relaxing and refreshing to get outside and enjoy nature.

"We always went for walks on the beach or in the woods," my friend Suzanne Perdew told me. They even walked in the rain! We don't usually get that energetic. Though we have gotten caught camping in the rain, being outside in the rain is not something we invite.

For Ardyce Earhart, walks with her father on Sabbath had special meaning. "In nice weather, Dad would take our family for a Sabbath-afternoon walk. I learned the names of plants and trees. It was one of the few times he had time for us because we lived on a farm, and there was a lot of work to do."

It would be nice to think that everyone has experiences like these on Sabbath, but in reality many families are divided over Sabbath observance. When spouses don't share convictions, it can create strife in the family.

Lorraine Owen, of Western Australia, told me about growing up and spending Sabbath attending afternoon meetings, walking in the park, having an afternoon nap, visiting church folk, or sometimes nursing homes to sing for residents. Then she met and married a non-Adventist and stopped going to church.

"When our children were ages six and three I realized I had to do something about their spiritual and eternal destiny," Lorraine says, "so I returned to church. It was a difficult time with World War III erupting every Friday evening and Sabbath morning. Having a family tradition with my own little family was almost impossible, although I did manage to keep the children occupied with Sabbath activities despite the telly going at times.

"Of course, there were the AJY's [Adventist Junior Youth] and Family Hour programs that were a blessing to keep the children involved in godly things, but I so much missed the ideal plan of the Sabbath being a special family blessing. I sometimes had mixed feelings about the Sabbath—part of me longed for each Sabbath and the blessings of worshiping God and meeting with God's people, and part of me dreaded it because with it always came tension and argument. Thankfully, after about four years my husband started to attend church and about a year later was baptized. Things improved and Sabbath was special all the time.

"But unfortunately, about four years ago, my husband lost interest in spiritual things again and stopped attending church. Things reverted back to the way it was years ago. Having family traditions is wonderful if you have been fortunate to be part of a family where there is unity in beliefs, but for some it is only a longed-for dream. I suppose you have come across many Christians with this same experience, and probably the percentage of people who could relate to these experiences would be high."

Of course Lorraine is right. For many people, keeping the peace ranks higher than creating traditions, out of need, not preference. When conducting Sabbath seminars, I have been asked what to do when living in a home where other family members are not converted. This is a hard question and one that doesn't have an answer wrapped up in a neat package, one-size-fits-all. How you observe Sabbath has a lot to do with what is going on in your home and your place in that home. It also depends greatly on how much resistance you encounter to your efforts.

To whatever extent it is possible, I suggest encouraging an unbelieving spouse to participate in your celebrations and traditions. Gaining his or her cooperation will accomplish a lot in the goodwill department. Beyond that, no one can be forced to participate. In that case, maybe your Sabbath traditions need to be carried on outside your home.

"Another tradition is the Sabbath afternoon lie down. Well, it is a day of rest now, isn't it?"
– LESLEY MCGRATH

Another special consideration when discussing Sabbath traditions is that while adults perceive the Sabbath hours to speed past all too quickly, for many children they stretch on endlessly. It becomes very important, therefore, to keep children interested and occupied. Sabbath "lay activities" are not going to appeal to the younger set. They've got too much energy to burn.

One thing we used to do on Sabbath before we had children, though I can see it appealing to them greatly, was "pet therapy." We would go to the local Humane Society and pick up a few puppies and kittens to bring to the local nursing home. You must arrange all this in advance, of course. At the nursing home we'd head off down the halls with our furry bundles, stopping by the residents' rooms for a short chat, letting them pet the animals if they wanted to. This accomplished two things: It provided socialization and companionship for the animals and brightened the residents' day.

"My sister began her family after my children were adults," Marian Forschler told me. "My husband and I worked hard to do all we could to make her two children feel important to us and much loved. When we visited from out of town, we made it a point to resist sleep and do things they would enjoy on Sabbath afternoon. One of the most loved Sabbath games was Bible charades. One time we had the two-year-old girl being the sheep and her four-year-old brother being the shepherd. Two-year-olds being what they are, the sheep soon chased the shepherd up the stairs on the bank in Grandma's backyard."

> *"After a cold-cereal breakfast with fresh fruit, we attend Sabbath School and church, invite guests for lunch; take a walk or read a book, depending on the weather; and have another special worship time."* —LINDA DOWNS

Games are popular with children. My friend

Suzanne Perdew and her family enjoyed playing Bible games on Sabbath afternoon when it was really raining. "Our favorite was Egypt to Canaan. We three kids would work on learning all the answers during the week, so if we had company we would always win!"

"As a family (my husband, me, and our children) we always tried to make Sabbath a special day for our children," says Emilie van Wyk. "This was a day that we did things together out in nature or in the house, depending on the weather. We tried to have something special to eat and special Sabbath games that we played on Friday evenings. Later, when the children were bigger, we had special family meetings on Friday evenings and discussed things that were dear to us. We laughed together and had a good time!"

Spending time together is the most important ingredient of Sabbath time. Reading together is one of our favorite ways of spending time together. My husband, Rob, is reading to the kids out of what we call the Blue Books, *The Bible Story* series by Arthur S. Maxwell. I think we enjoy it as much as the children do, and it has provoked many discussions about Bible stories.

Sonja Knight has a creative idea for making books. "I began this project with my four-year-old son Lane and my two-year-old son Luke. I have been saving any pictures from small to large that remind us of Jesus. They can be pictures from catalogs, books that are falling apart, calendars, etc. I keep pictures of animals, nature, people, and anything else that you can use in a discussion about Jesus and why He made them.

"Each Sabbath, we take an 8 1/2" x 11" blank page that can be of any color. Then we select pictures from our picture box and cut the pictures in different shapes and sizes. I even let Lane use a paper edger to give his pictures a special touch. We then glue our pictures onto our plain paper with glue sticks. Lane knows how to insert his finished page into a clear sheet protector and add it to his very own binder. On the outside of the binder we traced each child's hands and wrote his name and age. Soon they will have a book full of pictures that are fun to look at and learn from.

"I think it gives them a sense of satisfaction knowing that they made their own book. This is a good project for rainy or cold Sabbaths or for Friday evenings when the sun goes down early. Even during pleasant weather, you can do this with children who no longer need naps while their younger siblings sleep for an hour or two."

Kids enjoy socializing as much as adults do too. Laura Ames had a great idea that not only gave her daughter time to spend with someone her own age, it also strengthened her ties to her church by building relationships. "Our daughter is an only child," Laura says. "We tried to be sure that at least one Sabbath a month she invited a friend home for dinner. Then another Sabbath she was to invite someone she didn't normally associate with. We wanted her to get better acquainted with the other kids in her Sabbath School class. We tried to plan afternoon activities that kids enjoy: visits to a nature center, walks, bike rides (we lived in the country), or picnics outside."

As people shared with me their Sabbath traditions, I couldn't help but wonder how many more there were out there that we would never hear. Our traditions are something we should share with each other. Maybe you've never thought about it before, but the traditions you have as a family, no matter how elaborate, complicated, or downright simple they are, are important. Don't keep them to yourself. Share them with others so that we can all benefit in a ripple effect. Cherish your traditions and add to them when you can. Each one ties us to each other and to God. "The Sabbath should be made so interesting to our families that its weekly return will be hailed with joy." [1]

---

1. *The Faith I Live By,* Ellen G. White, p. 274.

Chapter Four

Sabbath Dinner

I have always enjoyed Adventist potlucks. I'll never forget the time, a few years after joining the Adventist Church, when my husband and I were traveling to my grandmother's house on a Sabbath. We stopped at a church nearby for worship. The entrance of the church was in the basement, which was filled with the aromas of food heating in the ovens in anticipation of potluck. I remember taking a deep breath and being filled with a sense of connection with all Adventists.

I realized that similar aromas were filling churches all across America. I could stop at any number of churches between the coasts and find Adventists preparing to share a meal together. It was an awesome moment when I sensed a unity that I had not realized before. I felt like part of a large, far-flung family. Even though I didn't know anyone in that particular church very well, I felt like I had come "home."

The Bible gave the breaking of bread special significance. In Revelation, Jesus says, "Here I am! I stand at the door and knock. If anyone hears my voice and opens the door, I will come in and eat with him, and he with me" (Revelation 3:20, NIV). One of the things Jesus was criticized for during His ministry was eating with "sinners." In some cultures social obligations are fulfilled in other ways until a host is comfortable enough to invite someone over for dinner.

A dinner invitation is not extended frivolously and, when received, is not taken lightly. For the cook, expending the time and energy in presenting a meal is a gift. The act of sharing a meal can be an intimate experience. If you've ever sat down at a table where you are uncomfortable, you will know what I mean. Tension around the table ruins appetites.

In Corinthians, Paul tells us that even in eating we should eat for the glory of God. "Whether you eat or drink or whatever you do, do it all for the glory of God" (1 Corinthians 10:31, NIV). Before this he warned, "Now I am writing to you that you must not associate with anyone who calls himself a brother but is sexually immoral or greedy, an idolater or a slanderer, a drunkard or a swindler. With such a man *do not even eat*" (1 Corinthians 5:11, NIV, emphasis mine).

Clearly, sharing a meal together is an intimate act in our relationship with others. It can strengthen the bond we share with them. Maybe years from now no one will remember just what they ate around your table, but they will always remember with joy the kindness and laughter that you shared. In light of this, Sabbath dinner holds a very special place in our week.

The early Christians are described in Acts as sharing meals. "Every day they continued to meet together in the temple courts. They broke bread in their homes and ate together with glad and sincere hearts, praising God and enjoying the favor of all the people. And the Lord added to their number daily those who were being saved" (Acts 2:46, 47, NIV). While we don't meet together at church and share a meal every day, we can certainly meet together once a week after church, either at a potluck or in our homes.

For some excellent Adventist potluck recipes, I refer you to cookbooks in this series: *Adventist Potluck Cookbook* and *Adventist International Cookbook*, both by Debby Wade, and *Sabbath Dinner Cookbook* (2 volumes) by Jacquelyn Beck, Jeanne Jarnes, and Kristen Jarnes.

"Potlucks were usually held at Battle Creek Academy," Sandra Cruz told me. "My parents always took a dish my mother had prepared the day before. Then one Sabbath, Mother was in England, and on Sabbath there was to be a potluck. On Friday, when Dad came home from work, he made a beautiful chocolate cake and as many pumpkin pies as my mom had pie plates for. He took the cake and pies to the potluck, and they were the best desserts there."

If one food attracted me to the Seventh-day Adventist Church, Special K® Loaf was it. I have a weakness for the stuff. Around here we call it K Loaf. Sharon Engel has developed a twist on the ever-popular Special K® Loaf.

"We usually have this loaf for Sabbath dinner. It is a little different from Special K® Loaf. My family likes it so much better. I have been making this for at least forty years. Of course we don't eat it every Sabbath. We really don't get tired of it. When we have been traveling or on vacation, we can't wait to get home and have some Cottage Cheese Loaf!" says Sharon.

Sharon Engel's Cottage Cheese Loaf

16 ounces cottage cheese
    (regular or low fat)
5 eggs
1 cube margarine
1 medium onion, chopped

3 packets G. Washington's® Golden Broth
1 13.5-ounce box of Kellogg's®
    Rice Krispies® cereal
Garlic salt to taste

Mix all ingredients well. Spray a 9" x 13" glass baking dish with cooking spray. Put the mixture into the pan and press down. Bake at 350°F for 40 minutes. Cut into squares. Serve with salad and cooked vegetables.

Maybe, like Lowell Litten, Jr., your family is large enough that getting together for a Sabbath dinner *becomes* a potluck. "When my great-grandmother was alive," Lowell told me, "we met weekly at her house for Sabbath potluck dinner. She had eight children, and they all lived in the same city. Most of their children (my aunts and uncles) also lived in the city, and so all of our cousins, grandparents, and family would meet after church services on Saturday at her house for lunch. Her kids even pooled their money and built on a huge banquet-sized room for the Saturday dinners."

I must admit that my favorite Sabbath company

entrées are those unmistakably Adventist in origin: Breaded Skallops®, Special K® loaf, hashbrowns and FriChik® loaf, "beef" stroganoff, or oatmeal patties. There's something comforting about these foods. They're like old family friends whose visits are looked forward to during the week.

Charles Reel's family celebrated birthdays during Sabbath dinner. "When I was growing up, we would have dinner with another family from the church either at their house or our house, and one of the

Ana's Hashbrown Casserole

My friend Ana Edison's hashbrown casserole is about as comfort food as food can get.

- 1 24-ounce package frozen hashbrowns (frozen diced potatoes in the freezer section of your supermarket)
- 1 10 3/4-ounce can cream of mushroom soup
- 1 cup sour cream
- 1/2 cup grated or chopped onion
- 4 ounces cheddar cheese, grated
- 1 can vegetarian diced chicken (I use FriChik®)
- 1 cup (2 cubes) butter, melted (I use 1/2 cup)
- 2 cups crushed cornflakes

Place hashbrowns on the bottom of an oiled 9" x 13" baking dish. Pour half the melted butter over them; then sprinkle cheese on top.

In a medium bowl, combine soup, sour cream, chicken, and onions; pour over the cheese. Top with cornflake crumbs that have been mixed with the remaining butter. Bake uncovered at 350°F for one hour.

Raphaëlle's Carrot Tofu

My friend Petrine Knight from Friendswood, Texas, shared a favorite recipe her mom makes for potluck.

- 2 tablespoons olive oil
- 2 small onions, chopped
- 3 tablespoons lemon juice or
    1 tablespoon lemon juice +
    2 tablespoons vinegar
- 3 or 4 cloves garlic, crushed
- 5 or 6 medium carrots, grated
- 2 16-ounce packages firm tofu, mashed until smooth
- Fresh parsley to taste
- 3 green onions, chopped
- 1 8-ounce package white button mushrooms, sliced
- Salt and other spices to taste (recommended: Lawry's Seasoned Salt or McCormick® Lemon and Herb Seasoning)
- 2 teaspoons low sodium soy sauce
- 1 to 2 tablespoons flour

In a large, deep saucepan or medium stock pot, sauté onion in oil. Add lemon juice or lemon juice/vinegar combination. Allow to reduce. Add garlic; let brown slightly. Add carrots; stir well. Spoon in tofu while stirring. When well combined, add parsley, green onions, mushrooms, salt, and other seasonings. Add soy sauce. Sprinkle with flour to thicken. Pour into flat baking dish; cover with foil. *Watch the temperature so the bottom doesn't burn.* Bake in 350°F oven for 20 minutes, or until top is brown and crisp.

---

things we would always do was celebrate whoever's birthday it was the previous week. The person or persons whose birthday it was usually got to pick the menu for that dinner also." You could do the same with any special occasion, such as welcoming new church members, dedicating a new baby, or honoring various groups: senior citizens, Sabbath School teachers, etc. What better time to celebrate the moments of our lives than during Sabbath dinner?

Whether you share your meal with family and friends or even visitors who attended church that morning, you will no doubt often share a meal with others. A few people wrote to tell me about wonderful meals and the experiences that went along with them, proving, to me at least, that food and fellowship make strong memories not easily forgotten.

"Growing up on a fruit farm in Lusaka, Zambia, our Sabbaths were always special," Jenny Holder told me. "Most of the church folk from the Lusaka SDA congregation joined us for lunch. This meant we would all go into the fruit orchards, equipped with a knife and move from tree to tree, making our choice of the best fruit. There were about six different types: mangoes, guavas, paw-paws, bananas, oranges, naartjies, avocado pears, etc. What wonderful Sabbaths we had—good fruit, good friends, and a long walk to the river in the afternoon!

"When I married and had my own little family, we decided to make our animals [pets] aware that the Sabbath was different from all other days by giving them a really special meal. This tradition is still in practice. My husband and son have since died, my daughter has moved away, and I am left with my dog and cat. Every Sabbath morning they get a special meal and a bit larger portion. I hope they have noticed that Sabbath is a special day!"

My friend Suzanne Perdew remembers the Sabbath lunches they had at home. "Our traditions included almost always having someone over for Sabbath lunch. We rarely got invited out. I don't know if it was because my dad was a dentist, or because he had three lively children! Whenever any visiting preacher or family came through town and visited our church, they came home for lunch."

"On Sabbath we always had dessert with lunch." —Lesley McGrath

---

Peggy Harris goes in for entertaining in a big way. "Growing up Adventist," she says, "on Sabbaths we would often have many guests. During World War II often there would be soldiers stationed nearby, new members, or guests passing through Sacramento, California, where we lived. I learned to love meeting new people and became comfortable with having many people as guests. Since I grew up that way, it was easy for me to do it as an adult in my own home.

"When my husband was stationed at Ft. Leonardwood in Missouri, we often had single SDA soldiers for the weekend. One time we even had the whole church of Waynesville over for Sabbath-afternoon dinner. It was a small church made up of about four families plus several army families."

Many people like Peggy are comfortable inviting people home to share a meal even if they don't know them. Although I have accepted dinner invitations from kind, generous folks like these, I have to admit, our family is not gifted in that way. And I believe entertaining those you don't know is a gift. Not all families have the personality for it in the same way that not all people have the same personality. This gift is a wonderful ministry for these families.

Diane Pearson, Dean of Women at Walla Walla College, grew up in a family that was certainly gifted. "Sabbath dinners were very special during my growing-up years. My father was an elder of our 60- to 100-member church for many of those years. He and Mom always invited the visiting pastor and any other visitors home for Sabbath dinner. Whether few or many, the visitors in our church did not leave without an invitation to fellowship around our table.

"There are memorable times. Once, Theodore Carcich (at that time the president of the Washington

Muriel Thompson's Sabbath Potato Salad

6 medium potatoes, peeled and cut into pieces
6 hard-boiled eggs
1/2 small onion or a few green onions, finely diced
Optional additions: finely diced celery, radishes,
   or other favored crunchy vegetables
   (NOTE: cucumber does not hold well overnight.)
Lawry's Seasoned Salt
Mayonnaise

Cook potatoes; cool. Dice cooled potatoes and eggs into large bowl. Add onion and celery or other fresh vegetables. Mix gently with large spoon. Sprinkle with Lawry's Seasoned Salt. Add several tablespoons mayonnaise; mix gently.

When mixed to suit your taste, cover; refrigerate until family meal is ready. *This salad can also be made a day ahead and stored covered in the refrigerator.*

Conference) told my parents that he would rather eat soup and sit on a wooden box at the table of members than to dine with the fanciest tableware and cuisine in a restaurant. He was able to sit on a chair when he visited us, but there were times when so many visitors came to our house that members of our family sat on wooden orange crates so that visitors could sit on our chairs. The tradition has been kept in our family by my siblings and me of showing hospitality to strangers and friends alike. We have made friends from many places by sharing a Sabbath meal with them. I am blessed more than they!"

If you'd like to start a family ministry by inviting visitors home, begin the way Diane's family did. Simply ask each one. Or you could follow the example of Judi Larsen of New Zealand. "I take the church phone list, start at the beginning and invite one or two families at a time (depending on the size of the families) for dinner. Sometimes I arrange it ahead of time, sometimes on the spur of the moment. I am a very busy person and don't always have time to cook extra on Fridays. What I do then is ask the person what they are planning to do for lunch and then suggest they bring what they've cooked and combine it with our food for lunch.

"I usually cook a rice dish in the electric skillet and supplement it with frozen vegetables, a can of baby corn, some sort of vegetarian protein, and flavor it with a packet of onion or mushroom soup mix and some soy sauce. Another Sabbath favorite is fruit crumble."

Lora Hendrickson, who home-schools her children in Pendleton, Oregon, tries to entertain once a month. "Sabbath dinners are usually simple meals to

JUDI LARSEN'S FRUIT CRUMBLE

2 cups rolled oats
1 cup whole-wheat flour
1/4 cup sugar

1/2 cup oil
1 teaspoon vanilla
2 quarts fresh or canned fruit of choice

Mix dry ingredients. Add oil and vanilla; mix until crumbly. *This crumble can be done in two medium baking dishes or one large one.* Place fruit in bottom of pan(s); cover with crumble topping. *Can be used as dessert after lunch or with ice cream and popcorn for a light supper.*

---

decrease work, but we try to have company for one week a month if possible. No one minds soup and bread at these meals; our visitors just love the fellowship and don't miss the prepared meat substitutes. Because our kids are home-schooling, any guest is a wonderful guest to have. Old or young, the kids enjoy them. We try to go to a church potluck about once a month for fellowship, too, and when life is pressing around us especially hard, we make sure to have days of "just us" Sabbaths too.

"In fact, there have been a few Sabbaths we've just skipped church to be together as a family, in the mountains or even at home, for the day. This might be considered 'un-Adventist' to some people, but we enjoy Family Sabbath in this sense to bring us together again."

It's one thing to contemplate having company over for dinner. You have plenty of time, then, to create your menu, to make changes, adjust quantities, and prepare for the meal so that everything goes smoothly. But what about those times when you invite someone on short notice or even home from church with you when you are completely unprepared to entertain? What then? What can you feed them?

The best preparation for the unexpected, is, of course, preparation for the unexpected. Which may sound redundant, but if you don't think about it now, you'll be surprised by it later. Having a well-stocked pantry is a must if you want to be capable of inviting company over on the spur of the moment. Keeping your pantry stocked with essential items will give you the freedom to enlarge your dinners to feed any number of hungry mouths.

I've come to the conclusion that there are two types of cooks: those who keep most foodstuffs on hand to meet every eventuality and those who buy something when the necessity arises and keep only the basics on hand. The second type will have trouble meeting the challenges of last-minute cooking. If you don't want to keep on hand ingredients that you use infrequently, consider at least stocking up on the ones you use most often.

Keeping several items in your pantry will make it easy to entertain at a moment's notice. While you may prefer to limit or exclude super-convenience items from your everyday table, some will prove invaluable when it comes to quick-and-easy meals. Instant mashed potatoes will easily coordinate with the ones you baked to extend that element of your meal. Quick-cooking rice can be mixed with any regular rice you may have precooked. Frozen vegetables will supplement the fresh ones you have already prepared.

BONNIE FOOTE'S GERMAN LASAGNA

Bonnie brought this lasagna to our most recent potluck and won rave reviews. See if it doesn't do the same for your guests.

3/4 cup butter or margarine
3/4 cup all-purpose flour
1 packet of G. Washington's® Golden Broth
2 teaspoons onion salt
2 1/2 cups milk
14 1/2 ounces broth (water + 2 teaspoons McKay's® Chicken Style Seasoning)

1 19-ounce can Saucettes®, drained and shredded
2 eggs
12 ounces small-curd cottage cheese
9 lasagna noodles
1 16-ounce can sauerkraut, rinsed and squeezed dry
2 cups Monterey Jack cheese, shredded and divided

In a saucepan, melt butter. Stir in flour, G. Washington's® Golden Broth, and onion salt until smooth. Gradually stir in milk and broth. Bring to a boil; cook and stir for two minutes or until thickened. Add Saucettes®; heat through.

In a separate bowl, combine eggs and cottage cheese. Spread 1 cup Saucettes® mixture in a greased 9" x 13" baking dish. Layer with three noodles, a third of the Saucettes® mixture, half the cottage cheese mixture, sauerkraut, and 3/4 cup cheese. Repeat layers. Top with the remaining noodles and Saucettes® mixture (dish will be full). Cover; bake at 350°F for 50 to 60 minutes or until bubbly. Sprinkle with remaining cheese. Bake 5 minutes longer or until cheese is melted. Let stand 15 minutes before cutting. Serves 12.

> *"One of my friends has a family tradition of serving spaghetti for Sabbath dinner each week. With teenagers in the home and a variety of church programs taking place, whichever family member arrives home first starts the spaghetti. The family also can bring home guests unannounced because it's easy to make more spaghetti."*
> —Faith Laughlin

You can expand a meal in several ways. Let's start with a spaghetti meal. Besides the main course of spaghetti, let's assume you have prepared a salad, garlic bread, a vegetable, and cookies for dessert. The amount you have prepared will feed your family. In addition, you invite a family of four over for dinner. You can creatively expand this meal in the following way:

First, add another can of sauce. If you don't have enough meatballs, break up the ones you have so the "meat" will be scattered throughout the sauce. Add a can of vegetarian burger if you feel it is still too skimpy and you have it in your stocked pantry. Open a bag of frozen vegetables and add it to what you have. If you don't have more lettuce and tomatoes to add to your salad, expand it by adding another green vegetable (spinach, collards, or cabbage), if you have it, or by adding additional salad ingredients (feta, shredded carrots, roasted sunflower seeds, black or green olives, broccoli, or cauliflower). If you have nothing with which to expand the salad, be sure you have plenty of vegetables.

To increase the bread if you don't have more Italian bread to make garlic bread, use any bread, or sliced up rolls, sprinkle with garlic powder, and toast in a moderate oven. While you are eating, put a can or jar of fruit in the freezer (don't forget it in there!).

WHERE'S-THE-BEEF? "MEATBALLS"

1 cup crushed cheese crackers
1/2 cup pecan meal
   (cashew meal works in a pinch)
1 small onion, grated
3 eggs

Garlic powder to taste
   (This is entirely subjective. I up-end the shaker and count to five.)
1/2 cup grated cheddar cheese
1/4 cup grated Parmesan cheese

Mix all ingredients; allow to cool in the refrigerator for at least 15 minutes. *The mixture can be refrigerated, tightly covered, overnight if you'd rather make your meatballs just before serving.* Form into walnut-sized balls (they will expand as they cook, so don't make them too big). Bake for 30 minutes at 350°F or fry them in oil. Once browned, place meatballs in a pot of spaghetti sauce; simmer over medium heat until ready to serve.

Serve this with whipped cream, if you have it, or sprinkled with cinnamon or nutmeg if you don't, with the cookies for dessert.

If your meal can't be enlarged, simply add side dishes to fill the empty plates. Side dishes of beans will make up for the smaller serving of protein. Chick peas are especially well suited for this. Toss them with a little olive oil, parsley, garlic, and salt to taste. (You can add a pinch of cumin too if you want to get adventurous.) Vegetable side dishes don't need to coordinate. Most vegetables mix quite nicely. If you are serving a vegetable such as steamed broccoli, you might consider roasting carrots to crispy tender for variety. Toss them with a little olive oil, sprinkle with the vinegar of your choice (white wine vinegar works well), and dust with dill. Roast the carrots in the oven for a quick, easy side dish. Stir them occasionally so they won't stick and burn.

Desserts can easily be stretched by adding an element like fruit, ice cream, or, in a pinch, boxes of Little Debbies®, which are always a hit. Doubling your meal can be a challenge, but if you approach it creatively, you will find many ways it can be accomplished. While the meal is important, the fellowship will always beat it hands down.

THE PREPARED PANTRY

Items to keep in stock so you will be ready to expand your meals at a moment's notice:

Spaghetti sauce
A variety of pasta
Instant mashed potatoes
Instant brown rice
A variety of frozen vegetables
Vegetable bouillon cubes
Canned tomatoes, fruit, and beans
Cans of prepared vegetarian meat substitute such as vegetarian burger, hotdogs, FriChik® or Swiss Stakes® are helpful to quickly and easily add protein to your table

---

Before we leave the subject of Sabbath meals, it's worth mentioning breakfast, the most important meal of the day. It seems Adventists also have a tradition of having special breakfasts on Sabbath. In our family my husband will often make pancakes, waffles, or crepes (we eat them Canadian style, slathered with butter, peanut butter, and maple syrup and layered like flapjacks.) I'm more apt to pick up croissants at the local bakery. And we often enjoy a large fruit salad. I'm partial to big family-style breakfasts on the weekends. Eggs, vegetarian sausages or Stripples®, and toast are often on the menu.

"One of the things I did with my kids on Sabbath mornings," says Marian Forschler, "was have a treat of some kind for breakfast. We planned it ahead of time, then went to the store and got it Thursday after school. We all looked forward to this."

Pat Moore's family came up with a special way to eat shredded wheat. "Another Sabbath special is Sabbath morning shredded wheat. Spread the large biscuit with creamy peanut butter. Sprinkle with brown sugar and bake in a toaster oven till the sugar begins to melt. Eat immediately. It crackles when you add milk! My kids still love it."

And some of us eat breakfast for supper on Sabbath. "On Sabbath evening we usually had a family over, and we ate homemade waffles with fresh or canned fruit," Dixie Plata remembers. "My dad would always make the waffles, using a very old-fashioned waffle iron. We still use that same one these more than forty years later."

Whatever you eat, however you eat it, with whomever you eat it, do it all for the glory of God. Your meals will be occasions to remember and will bless the lives of those you fellowship with. No matter what you have in your pantry, how elaborate or plain your table, how rich or simple your fare, the most important thing is the sharing and the fellowship.

Chapter Five

Saturday Night (a.k.a. Game Night)

My first encounter with this phenomenon—and a custom this unique can only be called a phenomenon—was when my family first began to attend the Adventist church in Williston, Vermont. My parents made friends with a couple there who were kind enough to often invite us over for dinner, as we lived an hour from church.

They played games on Sabbath and popped popcorn and coated it with nutritional yeast. (The yeast makes it taste a bit like cheese popcorn; I would suggest adding some garlic powder for a little zing.) The games I remember most were Egypt to Canaan and one that had something to do with shekels.

The evenings with that family gave us a little glimpse into the passion Adventists have for games. In light of the trend toward watching television and playing solitary video games, these family-oriented social times seem like reclaiming ground. We shouldn't underestimate their importance. Ellen White says, "But few realize the constant, wearing labor of those who are bearing the responsibilities of the work in the office. They are confined withindoors day after day and week after week, while a constant strain upon the mental powers is surely undermining their constitutions and lessening their hold on life."[1] My real introduction to "Game Night" came after I was married. Saturday night was the social event of the week. Crowds would flock to Rob's grandparents' or his parents' house. Food would be made and consumed. Games would be energetically played: Rook, Up and Down, Uno™, and Pit. We let the good times roll. I assumed this was just a family interest until my acquaintance with Adventists across the country broadened. I remember the time Maylan Schurch mentioned to me that Dutch Blitz was the game of choice in his area of the West Coast. And while I taught a summer course at Southern College, a friend from Tennessee introduced me to Kings, Queens, and Paupers. In this game you even get to wear hats! (Part of the profit from the sale of this game goes toward the purchase of property for a local church. To contact Debbie's Games write: Debbie's Games, 16625 Redmond Way, Ste. M412, Redmond, WA 98052.) One family favorite we've discovered is Domino Dice. Part of the appeal is that it's easy enough for our children (currently ages seven and four) to play.

A Few Saturday-Night Games

- Cupcake Walk. *Place numbered sheets of paper on the floor. Participants stand on the papers. There should be a couple sheets without numbers. The person in charge of the game starts the music. Players step from one paper to the next.*

When the music stops abruptly, they must scramble for footing on the paper closest to them. The person in charge draws a number out of a hat, and whoever is standing on that number gets to select a cupcake. They must sit out the rest of the game so there can be other winners. If no one is standing on the drawn number, there is no winner and the music starts again.

- Hobo Relay. *Relay to dress like hobo. Each person on the team adds another article to his or her outfit when they run to the clothes heap. We even let preschoolers play.*
- Piñata
- Raw-egg toss (outdoor activity)
- Tug-o-War over a kiddie pool in the center.
- Clothespin Drop. *Each player holds his or her arm out straight from shoulder and tries to drop twelve clothespins into a narrow-mouth quart jar.*
- Balloon Stomp.
- Old-fashioned hay ride into the country with corn roast/campfire at destination.

—SUBMITTED BY DONITA CULBERTSON

There's just something about getting a gang of people together to have fun that bonds them together. Anita Jacobs enjoys cooking for a crowd, and her family gets together for dinner and games. "We gather together a few family and/or friends. I'll prepare something like a Mexican supper (i.e., enchilada casserole and create-your-own burritos). Dessert might be a choice of fillings for cream puffs—lemon pudding or chocolate whipped cream.

"After sundown worship, supper, and cleanup, we bring out the double 12 dominoes and play Cardinal Mexican Train®. I think what I especially enjoy about this game is that anyone any age can play. Quite often the young children do as well, or better than, the adults. In the game you start with double 12. The next round is with double 11, down to the double blank. So it definitely takes up an entire evening!

"It is fun to have a table game that can involve all ages. We've had friends over, and their six-year-old son played with us. He did as well as the rest of us."

How to play
Cardinal Mexican Train®.

Here is an abbreviated version of the game for double 12s. You should find complete directions in your box. They also have double 15s now. So you'd start with the double 15 and work your way down to the double blank (that would be sixteen rounds).

If six to eight people are playing, everyone draws 12 dominoes that have been mixed face down. Whoever has the double 12 starts. Each person makes his own train beginning with a 12 to connect to the double. So if your train has a 12 and a 9, the next domino needs to connect with the 9, etc. So you want your train as long as possible. The "extras" in your hand that don't match in your train can be used on the Mexican train. The person who had the double 12 has the option of starting his own train or beginning the Mexican train (but only if he or she has more than one 12 as they don't want to ruin their train).

Everyone can play on the Mexican train, but you can only play on your own train if you don't have a domino to continue your train. Then you draw one domino, and if it can't be played on your train or the Mexican train you are "open," and anyone can play on you until it is your turn again. If you play on your train, it is "closed," and no one can play on you. If you play on the Mexican train, but not on your own when your train is "open," your train remains open. Putting a button or penny on the end of the train signifies that the train is closed.

Each person plays one domino per round unless he or she has a double; then it is necessary to play another domino. *Our rule is that if I play a double on the Mexican train, I can then play either on the Mexican train or my own train. If I don't have a domino to play, I have to draw one. If I still can't play, then the next person has to play on that double. If he can't (and he can draw one domino), then he is open, etc. around the circle. (Sometimes it can really mess up people's* trains because once a train is open, anyone can play on it.)

Play ends when someone has used up all his or her dominoes.

Scoring: We just count the number of dominoes left in each person's hand. The lowest score at the end of all the rounds is the winner. Some people play that you count all the spots of the dominoes in your hand, and that is your score.

This may sound complicated, but it really isn't. When the double 12 is on the table, each person has a "corner" of the domino closest to them to begin their train. The Mexican train is started away from that, and someone close to it serves as "engineer" to keep the dominoes straight.

If you are playing with a group of more than

eight people, draw fewer dominoes—fewer people, draw more. If no one has the highest double (12 or 15) to start, each person draws one more until someone draws the double. I like having lots of dominoes as it makes it easier to have a long train because you have more numbers to work with.

—Directions kindly provided by Anita Jacobs

Terry and Tammy Cantrell from Newbury Park, California, like to have a "Soup and Something Party." "You either bring a crock-pot full of your favorite soup or 'something' to go along with it (like crackers, bread, cornbread, fruit, etc.)," they told me. "Then we have a great soup potluck and then play games for two or three hours afterward. We rotate whose house we go to so that no one family always has to clean the house or be the ones to cook. It is great fun! Our favorite group games are Mad Gab, Taboo, Guesstures, Turkey Foot (with colored dominoes), Catch Phrase, and Pit."

Traveling socials are fun too, where the entertaining is divided among several houses. Jenny Lowe said the kind she liked is called a traveling tea. "We would have, say, beverages and snacks at the first house, then soup at the second house, the main course at the next house, and dessert and games at the last house. These teas have always had a good attendance."

Our young people love the socializing that game nights and socials provide. My young friend, Petrine Knight, from Texas says it very well. "We used to have a lot of socials at our old church. We'd have vespers and then close Sabbath and party! We'd have themes, like for Valentine's Day we'd go out to Olive Garden and eat. Then we'd go to someone's house and play games such as matching famous couples and stuff and just have fun. Then we'd have a 'go western' social where we'd dress cowboy/cowgirl style and bring chili and other western food. We'd eat and play games, people would sing, and we'd tell stories and pop popcorn. Then we'd have a 'sixties' social, and so on. It was really cool because then we'd all be ourselves, and not stuffy church people, and have a ton of fun. And for vespers and at socials Pictionary® was the game! It was too fun!"

"Some of the most memorable Saturday-night parties," Diane Pearson told me, "have been with our entire church group—all generations. The elderly love to have relay races with balloons or walking with paper boxes for shoes or dressing up in unique clothing just as much as the younger ones. Popcorn

---

Here are some dips that would mix well with your next Saturday Game-Night Party. These recipes are from the kitchen of my friend Rachel Kinne.

CHEESE DIP

8 ounces white American cheese, cubed
1 cup half-and-half (more or less as desired)
Canned jalapeño peppers, diced

Melt cheese with half-and-half in a double boiler over low heat. Add jalapeños to taste. Serve warm as dip for corn chips. *Dip will thicken as it cools.*

Chocolate Fondue

3 7-ounce bars Toblerone® Milk Chocolate
2 cups miniature marshmallows
1 12-ounce bag milk chocolate chips
1 pint heavy cream
1 teaspoon vanilla extract

Place ingredients in crockpot to melt and simmer on very low heat for two or three hours.
IDEAS FOR DIPPING: apple, banana, or fresh pineapple slices; grapes; marshmallows; pound or angel food cake; shortbread; butter cookies; strawberries, raspberries, or blueberries.

Sweet-and-Sour Dip

1 20-ounce can crushed pineapple
1 18-ounce jar apricot preserves
1/2 cup prepared mustard
Vegetarian sausages, cut into pieces

Mix first three ingredients in a saucepan; heat just until bubbling. Reduce heat and simmer for 10 minutes or so. Prepare the vegetarian sausage by browning. Just before serving, put vegetarian sausage pieces into the sweet-and-sour dip. Use toothpicks or fondue skewers to retrieve from pan.

---

and apples can't be beat for Saturday-night nibblings."

Melinda Sherman from Caldwell, Idaho, sub-

mitted a fun activity that younger children can enjoy if some of the games for the group are too advanced for them. She makes edible playdough that can be colored, flavored, and shaped numerous ways and then eaten by the young artists.

Schools can get in on the fun too. In fact, if you live near one you can probably take advantage of the programs they will offer. If not, take the party to your house. "When I was in the seventh and eighth grades,

EDIBLE PLAYDOUGH DESSERT

1/2 cup cornstarch
3 3/4 cups confectioners' sugar
1 1/4 cups cake flour

1 8-ounce package cream cheese, softened
Food coloring, as desired
Natural or artificial flavoring, as desired

In a bowl, combine first three ingredients. Cut in cream cheese until the mixture resembles coarse crumbs. Divide into separate bowls if you want several colors and/or flavors. Add food coloring and/or flavorings, as desired; mix well with a spoon. The playdough should then be ready for *clean* hands to shape it into edible desserts.

TIPS: A great chocolate brown color can be achieved by adding the following ingredients: 1 part cream cheese, 3 parts cocoa powder, 2 parts cornstarch

If playdough is ever sticky, add a little more cornstarch and mix well. You can make flat, stackable desserts (as in the photo at the beginning of this chapter, p. 68) by arranging the playdough on a plate, covering the playdough with plastic wrap, then lightly pressing another plate of similar shape into it.

every Saturday night unless there was a program at the academy, we had a party at our house," Sandra Cruz remembers. "We just played games and my folks made Chex® Mix and we had Hawaiian punch to drink. The Chex® Mix was served in small paper cups."

The essence of Saturday-night games is socializing.

Games provide that element of fun and interaction most of us lack on a daily basis. If your family or church isn't involved in some type of Saturday-night games, start your own tradition!

---

1. *My Life Today,* Ellen G. White, p. 206.

Recipes for Chex® Mix abound. Check the Chex® cereal boxes or run a search online where you'll come up with lots of varieties of the famous snacking mix. Here's something a little different to try at your next Game Night get-together.

OYSTER CRACKER SNACKERS

1 package ranch salad dressing mix
 (I use Hidden Valley Ranch® Original)
1/4 to 1/2 cup salad oil
 (I use extra virgin olive oil)

1/2 teaspoon dill weed
1/2 teaspoon garlic powder
5 cups plain oyster crackers

Combine the salad-dressing mix, oil, dill, and garlic powder. Pour over crackers; mix well to coat crackers. Place on cookie sheet; bake at 250°F for 15 to 20 minutes, stirring gently while baking so they won't stick.

CHAPTER SIX

FAMILY TIES

Many Adventist families developed traditions to show love and support for others in the family circle. Many of these traditions began when their children left home for boarding school. Other traditions grew out of the desire to keep in close touch with family members who live too far away to visit often. Still other traditions grew around celebrations of life milestones.

Although not an Adventist at the time, I did attend an Adventist boarding academy for one year, so I know a little about the angst of leaving home at a young age. Many Adventist young people live away from home to attend school at some point. Adventist parents don't opt out of parenting during school months though. So many of you wrote me with wonderful, creative ways to maintain and strengthen the bond with your kids during the school year.

Some of the ideas were social. "One of the things

my mom did fairly often was bring a couple of half-gallons of chocolate ice cream, 7UP®, glasses, and spoons down to academy," Marian Forschler says, "and my sister and I would gather in one of our rooms and we'd all have 7UP® floats. My, but they tasted good. My mom got to know a lot of our friends and even took some of them under her wing—some of them needed mothering and either didn't have mothers or had inattentive or inadequate mothers. I always felt good that our friends liked our mom so much. My mother is ninety-one now, and she still remembers many of my academy friends."

Frequent visits aren't always possible because of distance between the home and the school. "When my daughter was in academy, we had a tradition that we would always phone on Wednesday night after prayer meeting," Ginger Harvey told me. "We would talk about each others' week and would pray for each other. We'd pray about anything she felt was important, such as events that were coming up or a test that she was going to take (I would also pray for her on the day of her test). We would always, and still do, end the call with the words, 'I love and miss you very much.'

"About twice a month I would send cookies or call the nearest florist and have them send a bouquet of flowers to her. On Valentine's Day my husband always sent her a dozen red roses. He still does this. On her birthday just the two of them would go out to dinner, and he would buy a flower for her to wear."

Frequent communication of love and caring is so important, even for kids who appear not to want it or seem to have grown "beyond" it. I was a kid like that, the independent type. But the homesickness that comes over you when you're away from home can be hard to deal with. Even the brave ones who put up a good front need that support from home. This is particularly true during times when other kids might have the opportunity to visit home or relatives who live nearby.

"My daughter Stephanie was home-schooled for two-and-a-half years," Christine Greene told me. "As part of our day, we had morning worship and worked on reading the Bible through together. We are very close, and it was a nice time for us. The first year she went away to Blue Mountain Academy in Pennsylvania, two hours from our home in Maryland, the shared devotional time stopped. Stephanie had major homesickness that just would not go away. In fact, a lot of the girls that year had a hard time with homesickness. We really wondered what to do, because she had begged to go to academy and had agreed that she would not quit and come home, even if she felt like it. The homesickness went on for weeks.

"One morning, the providential thought came over me that I should do the Bible reading with her over the phone each morning. I asked if she would like to try that idea. She agreed willingly. By the end of the week, her homesickness had all but disappeared. She told me that it was the Bible reading that made the difference, and she felt so much better. My daughter is a sophomore now, and we have our morning worship together at 6:10 a.m. each day. It has made a world of difference."

"We were fortunate that our sons did not have to leave home until they went to college," says Rosalia Coffen. "But once they were away at college, we called them each Sunday at a set time. We usually talked for about an hour to our older son. We found it helpful to be able to encourage him, especially at the beginning of each semester, when he would always seem to be overwhelmed, until he could get into the new schedule. For the first year, the weekly phone calls took the place of letter writing. By his second year, we had a computer, so we sent him an individualized version of the letter we were sending to our parents. And he appreciated that added reminder from home.

"When our second son left home, he told us we could still talk to the older one for an hour because he wouldn't have anymore than ten minutes of things to talk about. We were rather amused that often he would have more to say than his older brother. The Sunday phone call became such an important routine that it continued while our sons were in graduate school. Even though our sons are now married, the tradition continues: their wives want the tradition to include them—and now our first grandchild as well.

For us, letters and emails just don't replace hearing their voices. Our younger son preferred the snailmail to email when in graduate school. He just wanted something personal in the mail box, beyond the bills and junk!"

I agree wholeheartedly that email lacks the personal touch of letters and phone calls. Sure, it's convenient and can be used when times are rushed, but don't substitute it for calls or letters. Email lends itself to short updates and should be appreciated for what it is. Keep the personal touch. Let your fingers do the walking or send your love by pony express. Like Rosalia, you might find that the communication tradition you create when your children are away at school continues when they have families of their own. The Van Arsdales's tradition did.

"Our youngest son was the first to attend boarding

academy," Rick and Marion Van Arsdale told me. "The two older ones had lived at home when they attended academy. We would call him Friday night just before he would go to vespers, or if he had a busy schedule, he would call us to say Happy Sabbath. Most of the time it was a happy call, but sometimes if there was a problem or something bothering Andy, we would be able to talk it out with him.

"When his older sister left for college and then lived on her own, there was always the Friday-evening Happy-Sabbath call. Tammie now works in the health profession, and when she works Friday night, the call is often earlier. But keeping the phone line busy to say, 'Happy Sabbath, how was your week? Have a good Sabbath,' just makes the beginning of the Sabbath special, and it keeps the family connected even though they are miles apart.

"We have found that even after the kids are married, the Friday-evening calls continue. It makes the family ties stronger and the day the Lord set apart for Him and family a little more special. We discuss the week, good and bad, counsel, laugh, and just connect as only families can do. We have enjoyed the little tradition we began to keep in touch with our kids. It has become very special and brought the family closer together."

Investing time and effort into your family relationships will always pay rich dividends. It can take creativity and planning to find ways of showing love and support for your children in the routine and rush of ordinary life. But it's one of the most important things you can ever do for your kids.

Terry Koch and his wife Terri make it a priority too. "My wife and I have written a message to our two sons on the first day of the school year every year since they began in first grade. They are now both well into their college years. The messages are reminders of our love, our prayers for blessings in the school year just beginning, for our sons' reliance on God, and for Him to continue to be a growing presence in their lives.

"We were out of the country helping my brother with a series of Bible meetings in Estonia when our elder son first went to college. We returned about a week after school had begun and went to the dormitory where our son was living.

"We explained to the dean that we wanted to leave the annual message for our son in his room because we had been away when school had begun. The dean was intrigued by our request and personally accompanied us as we went to our son's room and left our message under his pillow. Apparently, it made a lasting impression on the dean, because he mentioned it to us when we saw him some time later.

"It seems as if our children are with us such a short time before they are established in their own lives, careers, and homes. How pleasant it is to provide them with waymarks of our support and love as they mature throughout their educational experiences."

CARE PACKAGES

Nothing quite says home like some of Mom's cookies or a cartoon from Dad. For me it was taking back some of Mom's Baco-bit quiche from a rare visit home. Here are a few ideas for assembling a care package.

Some Tips to Individualize Care Packages

- Buy a plain cardboard box and cover it with sayings, encouragements, cute stickers, etc. to

embarrass and delight them.
- Tape little notes to each item in the care package.
- Ask them from time to time what they miss or need and make a list of those items. When possible, include the items they request.
- Remember the roommate. One mother sewed an Advent calendar for her daughter and her daughter's roommate. She numbered the pockets and filled them with goodies. Those girls could barely wait to see what the next day's surprise would be.

What to Include in a Care Package

- Stationery and stamps
- Homemade cookies/brownies
- Rental certificates from the video store
- Small picture frames (they're always taking pictures of new friends)
- Interesting clippings from your hometown newspaper
- Magazines (always appreciated)
- Hanging air fresheners for automobiles (works great in dorm closets)
- Gum, breath mints
- The season's candies (Christmas, Valentine's, Easter, etc.),
- A new CD
- Gift certificates for fast-food restaurants
- Packets of instant hot chocolate
- Microwave popcorn
- Prepaid long-distance calling cards
- Holiday room or door decorations
- Instant soups (anything that can be made quickly with boiling water)
- School supplies

- Soap
- Shampoo
- Detergent (Repackage into recloseable plastic bags so shipping isn't so expensive.)
- Cold medicines
- Mugs or cups and saucers so that student can share the riches!
- A can of WD40 (No one will ever have a problem with squeaky door hinges.)
- Bus/train tokens
- Package of all-occasion cards

Party in a Box

My friend Liz created a unique birthday present for a daughter who could not come home for her birthday. "When our daughter's birthday arrived, I realized it would be the first one we would miss celebrating as a family. She was not one to announce to others, 'Say, it's my birthday next week,' so we decided to help her out! We sent a small box wrapped up as a present, and she was told to open it IMMEDIATELY! It contained an instant birthday party! We included napkins, balloons, candles, paper plates, streamers, and other things, including money to buy a decorated cake, ice cream, and punch! There was a banner also that said, LAURIE'S BIRTHDAY PARTY IS MARCH 7TH, AND YOU ARE INVITED! She put the banner on her door, and she had a great birthday! We all enjoyed it from afar!"

If you live close by, you can drop in and decorate the room and leave goodies behind: cake or cupcakes, punch, popcorn and popper, snack mix. Decorate the door with a banner and balloons announcing the birthday.

Care packages are not the only way to encourage

dorm students and remind them that the family back home loves them. Jean Boonstra's friend, Yvonne Higgins, has a clever way to remind her daughters that they are special to her.

"Yvonne has two daughters who are away at school, one in university and one in academy. Before they leave each fall, she makes them a pair of pajamas in a cozy fleece or flannel fabric. She does this so they'll think of home at night. Apparently, all of their friends in the dorms love the pjs and want Yvonne to make them some!"

Of course, kids away at school aren't the only ones who need to be nurtured. Kids living at home need rituals that provide time for communication and bonding. Marian Forschler addressed this need with a family cuddle.

"My kids used to pile onto my bed with me in the evening (I was a single parent for a while), and we'd read and talk about ideas and issues even though they were just in the early elementary grades. After I remarried, they often crawled into bed with me and my husband on weekend mornings, and we'd have nice, relaxed visits.

"We'd share ideas and make plans. I found that asking them for the reasons behind their ideas opened them up a lot, and I was able to know more about what was going on in their lives. I found it important not to laugh at their ideas or logic and to treat their ideas and thoughts with respect."

Sometimes it is grandchildren you want to invest your love in. Anna May Radke Waters has a wonderfully creative way to do this. "My grandparents all passed away either before I was born or shortly thereafter, and I always felt cheated. I wrote an autobiography of my life for our grandchildren, and included a biography of my husband, their grandpa, as well, so they will know us as we were before they were born. I included pictures of us when we were young.

"When our grandchildren, who are very scattered geographically, were young, we always gave them a gift certificate at Christmas time for two weeks at 'Camp Grandma.' The following summer, they would spend time with us, doing the things they enjoyed, such as playing games and miniature golf, baking bread and cookies, and going to the beach. We had wonderful times together and built many, many memories. Now they are all old enough to have summer jobs, Camp Grandma is in operation whenever they have time for a visit, even for just a weekend.

"Just for the fun of it I made a 'Grandma credit card' that was good for things like cookies and games. One ongoing thing I do for our grandchildren is to write an 'Update from Grams and Gramps' about once a month. In the Update I share what we are doing, as well as sharing the news of each of them with each other. In these Updates I also send copies of a favorite cartoon strip about an elderly couple that do some humorous things and remind me of my husband and myself. The kids love these cartoons, and it gives them a good laugh as well. It has been wonderful to build a special relationship with each one."

Lora and Cliff Hendrickson of Pendleton, Oregon, have found a way to communicate with their children about important, and sometimes emotional, issues families must deal with. "Family council is the most important thing we are working on. We have a ceramic jar on the piano in which anyone can put a note listing a concern or problem he or she wants to work on. Whenever there is a note in the jar, we make an appointment to talk as an entire family within the next few days. The person who wrote the concern has all the time he or she needs to talk without interruption. We've been able to make difficult changes much easier this way, discussing issues calmly after my husband, Cliff, and I have talked about the issue at length. (Cliff and I can also put issues in the jar, of course!)"

My friend, editor/author Penny Wheeler, shared with me a couple wonderful traditional games she plays with her kids. Try them with yours!

Just Because I'm Older

Noelle and I have a little routine that we've been doing since she was a child. (She's now a young adult.)

"I love you," I say to her.
"I love you better," she says.
"I love you best," I say.
But she has the last word: "Only because you're older and you've had more practice."

Squeeze Language

My mother taught my sister and me this routine. It's done by holding hands and alternately squeezing. No talking at all is allowed.

Three squeezes: (I love you.)
Four squeezes: (I love you too.)
Two squeezes: (How much?)
One giant squeeze. As a child I'd put all my strength in it, groaning and grunting, trying to show how much I loved my mother.

Times apart can be one of the challenges faced by families where one or both parents are required to travel for work. Creating ways to "keep in touch" with family members when you will be away lets them know that they are important to you. "I work part time as a nurse," Lisa Whitlow told me. "On the days that I work, I leave a note for the kids and my husband, telling them that I love them and will miss them. I often leave some kind of a treat. When my husband has to go out of town on business (he is the conference youth director), I give him a stack of cards with a specific day written on the envelope so that he can open a card from me each day that he is gone. He does the same for me. Besides the cards, we talk on the telephone morning and night. We hate to be apart!"

I often travel to speaking appointments or book promotions. Having to leave my children crying at the airport is heart wrenching. To soften the pain of separation, I've devised a "program" for when I'm away. Weeks before I leave on a trip, I begin collecting small items that can be mailed in cards. I also buy special cards (this is not a time to consider expense) for Rob and the kids, ideally one for each day I will be traveling. I address and stamp these cards ahead of time because I know I will be busy once I'm on the road. On the outside of the card I pencil in the day I intend to mail it.

Before I leave, I also record some books on tape so the children can listen to me read to them. This can backfire, depending on how old your children are. Rob said the first time I did this, Rachel heard my voice on the tape player when she woke up and ran into the living room, thinking I was home already.

To make the children's ride home from the airport

happier, I tell them, just before I board the plane, that I've left them something special on their pillows. It gives them something to look forward to on the way home.

Of all the ways to show that we care for our families, being there is probably the most important. The popular excuse for spending little time with family is that the quality of the time matters more than the quantity. But I think for family relationships it's a combination of quality and quantity of time that matters.

Lorene Beaulieu's family has made a commitment to "be there" for each other. "Our family decided to be at every important event for each other. This meant all graduations, special honors events, whatever was important enough that we needed each other's support. When we lived in the mission field, our daughter graduated from the academy. We flew our oldest son to Singapore to attend this event. He had just graduated the year before from Loma Linda University, and we all had attended his graduation.

"Our children went to different universities. We all met for each child's graduation, even from graduate school, no matter where we lived. We are scattered all over the United States—so it takes planning and effort to attend important events. We also talk with each child every week for as long as needed—no matter the cost. It has paid off in so much love and understanding between each of us and now between the in-laws who have joined our family and its traditions."

"I have given a number of seminars on family traditions because I think it's so important. Traditions are a bond that ties your children to your heart, to your beliefs, and to your church.

We need to celebrate! Even when we're gone, those traditions still remind them of their roots, even if they aren't walking that way right now."
—Linnea Torkelsen, Alumni and Development Director at Upper Columbia Academy

Baptism

Last year our family attended the baptism of two special friends, Darren and Matthew Manzari. The brothers were baptized in a remote part of an Adirondack lake. All the baptism attendees hiked in to the site. Talk about a festive occasion! It made such an impression on our son Joshua, that he decided when he is old enough, he wants to be baptized in a mountain lake too.

Baptism is an important milestone in our spiritual lives and deserves to be treated as such. Everyone remembers your birthday; isn't the day of baptism even more important? Some families think so, and they've come up with creative ways to honor it.

"On the anniversary of their baptisms, I have given my children a card or note of encouragement," says Joyce Brown. "I do this for several reasons. They need to know that I am praying for them continually. I think it is a good way to renew the vows of commitment to the Lord that they took at the time of their baptism. They look forward to this reinforcement and reconnection. It has been seventeen years for my son and twelve for my daughter since they were baptized. They look forward to receiving this special note from Mom each year."

Lisa Whitlow came up with a clever way to commemorate baptisms. "For my son Andrew's baptism at the camporee at Oshkosh, Wisconsin, I embroidered his name, the date, and place on the handkerchief that his dad, a pastor, used to baptize him with. I have an Adventurer in my club who will be baptized this month, and I am doing a handkerchief for her. I plan to embroider one for any other kids in my club, as well as my other two children when they are ready for baptism. I thought that this would make a neat keepsake of a special event!"

The Torkelson family believes that though baptism happens only once, it should be treated with the same importance as a wedding or graduation. "We believe that baptism is the most important event in our child's life," Linnea says. "We spend big bucks on bridal showers, baby showers, graduations, etc., but ordinarily we spend little or nothing on celebrating a baptism—we just sandwich it in between the offering and the special music at church. Here's how our family decided how to celebrate the children's baptisms: Let your child choose the most important place he or she can think of for being baptized. Our oldest chose our favorite beach in Hawaii, where we had previously lived. So we bought airline tickets and had the baptism in Hawaii.

"Expense should no more be an issue in planning a baptism than when planning a wedding or graduation. We invited the teachers that she'd had in Hawaii to be there. We invited friends, who we asked to be her prayer guardians, joining us in spiritual warfare to keep the devil at bay. They brought leis, cards, and ukuleles to sing praises; she chose the minister (dad) to baptize her; and we took pictures to chronicle the event just like we will her bridal shower and her baby showers in years to come.

"Our youngest chose the church as her favorite place. The same kind of invitations went out—

printed and special. We hosted a special dinner party at our house afterward; there were gifts and great joy.

"Now, every year on the baptism anniversary, we provide the flowers for church with a note in the bulletin saying that we are celebrating the best decision of our daughter's life and thanking Jesus for the good work He is completing in her. If we are not going to be at our home church, Dad buys an armload bouquet to present on that Friday night at worship. It is a chance to remind them of that special day—and to let them know that their parents and God have not forgotten that precious promise they made. We will continue this tradition every year till the day we die. If a child should choose not to continue walking with the Lord, the flowers will still come, because we are in the habit of doing it on that date. It would then be a gentle reminder that Jesus is still there for them, as we are. We have also committed ourselves as spiritual parents for the children who were baptized with our children and try to send a card or letter on the anniversary of their baptisms.

"Our friends' kids were baptized on Fourth of July Sabbath. They had a big picnic in their backyard to celebrate the baptism and a hike and other activities until it got dark; then had a great time with fireworks. Their parents were wise enough to point out to them that the Fourth of July in the United States is a celebration of freedom, just as baptism is a celebration of freedom from the bondage of sin. So now every time those kids see fireworks, their parents hope they will be reminded of the spiritual connection as well."

Equally important religious milestones are dedications of babies and young children. The event needs to celebrated, as well. Lori Bazan shared with me the traditions her family has for dedications. "Our family traditions for births has been to dedicate our newborn babies in our home church. We've always invited close friends and immediate family members to be present at all our nieces' and nephews' dedications. Following the dedication we always had a potluck luncheon to celebrate the dedication of our baby to God and our commitment to rear our child in a Christian environment, teaching him or her about God's love."

Adventist families have developed numerous traditions that remind their children and grandchildren that they are loved and cherished. Many of these traditions begin when the children are small and continue, sometimes in an adapted form, into their adulthood. Others begin when the children leave home for boarding school. Whatever the traditions, they support, encourage, and inspire.

CHAPTER SEVEN

CAMP MEETING

My camp meeting experience is limited. Our conference holds its camp meeting at Freeport, Maine. For us, that means four hours of driving one way for a weekend. When we attend, we rent a motel room. Every year I say I'd like to go for the entire week and stay on the grounds in a canvas tent. Someday, someday. . . .

Great speakers are one of the biggest draws during camp meeting. I was bitterly disappointed the year I had to miss hearing Clifford Goldstein because I was busy having a baby. I did, however, send one of his books along with Rob's parents to be autographed. I loved the camp meeting memories people sent me because they are how I imagine it would be to stay at camp meeting for the entire week.

"I remember the time it hadn't rained all summer," recalls Sandra Cruz. "When Elder H. M. S. Richards, Sr., came on the last weekend, he prayed for rain.

That night it rained all night, and all the trailers got stuck in the mud. It was even announced in the newspapers that it rained because of his prayer. That evening, my parents made me sit with them instead of going to the children's meeting. I kept my head down the entire time, but it was the first time—I was twelve years old—that I understood what a good speaker he was."

"I wasn't crazy about camp meeting," my friend Petrine Knight told me, "because all the little kids from other churches would 'steal' our Sabbath School rooms. I haven't been to a real tent camp meeting in years. Then camp meeting was just on Sabbath for a couple of weeks in a row, and they'd have this huge tent in the back lot. The grass would be all wet and squishy, and there were mosquitoes; but the speaker was always nice. Then afterward there would be the ABC book sale, which I always loved! Camp meeting was special in part because it was so different from weekly worship at church." Petrine bought my first book, *Playing God,* at one of those ABC book sales. That's how we met.

I loved the book sales even before I became a presenter at them. I would go with my list clutched in hand and a tiny budget in my pocket. I bought as much as I could afford, being one of those people who buys books first and things like food and clothing only if there is any money left over. The sales were exciting, and I was so thrilled to have a pile of books to take home that I never even minded the long hot wait in line for my turn at the cash register.

"I can remember Eric B. Hare's Michigan camp meeting stories to all the 'nasty children' in the

audience (i.e., us.) We were very proud of ourselves and our 'nastiness.' We were 'nasty' because we laughed at the tragic parts of his stories. Of course we couldn't help laughing; he made the stories hilarious." —Sandra Cruz

---

I hope this camp meeting book sale tradition isn't endangered as Kent Thomas of North Dakota suspects. "One grand tradition that seems to be dying is the annual ABC camp-meeting book sale," he told me. "It used to be such a big deal, but now it seems to be getting less and less important. I think that is unfortunate. Do you remember the days of sitting through a three-hour ABC camp meeting Sunday sale to get your case of FriChik®?"

I don't remember food being sold (I was concentrating on the books), but it would indeed be a shame if the book sales died out. They're a great social event, if nothing else, and most presenters work hard to infuse the sale with enthusiasm as well as great deals.

The Hendricksons in Oregon attend a different kind of camp meeting. This concept, family camp meeting, intrigues me. "We go to a family camp meeting with Restoration International, a family ministry that focuses on the basics of the gospel," Lora Hendrickson told me. "This camp meeting is not at all traditional, because the kids sit with their parents during the meetings and learn family concepts too! The two families who founded the ministry have children who are now teens/young adults, but through the years they have also been part of the families' speaking ministry. The kids speaking has been a special blessing to our children. It is a lot of work to sit in meetings most of the day, but we invest in it every chance we get."

"The best part of camp meeting for me," says Rosalia Coffen, "when I was growing up, was camp pitch and camp strike with my pastor father. It was a special time of socialization with the other pastors' children. But the bookstore was always very special.

"I enjoyed being able to push the pastors' babies around in a stroller when I was a teenager. At the Michigan camp meeting, I enjoyed the music that was piped all over the campground to encourage people to get up in time to attend the early-morning devotional. I often went alone as a teenager. I had two younger brothers that needed to be cared for, and my dad had other duties, so I was the only one free to go. My mother always made camp-pitch time special for us too. At no other time did she ever have so much time to spend with us. It was an opportunity to do some crafts together as well."

Alison B. Carleton, a busy physician, wife, and mom, sent me her fabulous memories of the Soquel camp meeting. This is the way I imagine camp meeting to be.

"I still have the five-drawer wooden dresser that sat in my closet until my family and I went to camp meeting each year when I was a young girl," she recalls. "My daughter Grace uses it now. But it still reminds me of packing for camp meeting, the smell of the grass, the cool, foggy mornings, warm afternoons in the golden canvas tent, and a simpler time when all I needed for a week would fit in one of those drawers.

"We packed our clothes in the five dresser drawers. My brothers and I got one drawer each and Mom got two. Dad put the drawers in the trunk of the car with other things we didn't want to get dusty. It was always sunny as we swept out the yard trailer and loaded it with the frame of the dresser, an ice chest, a folding table, cots, chairs, a pole to tie to the middle tent rail to hang our clothes on, and a piece of old rug to cover the bare board floor. Dad covered it all with a tarp.

"Dad drove us up to Soquel in the coastal Santa Cruz Mountains and helped us arrange our stuff in the tent. The tents were pitched in rows and tied to each other. They were twelve-feet square with four six-foot square floorboards. Two cotton mattresses and two metal cots with folding legs came with each tent. The cots just fit the length of a floorboard. Dad and Mom would try to level and steady the floorboards some, put down the rug and arrange the two cots, being very careful not to pinch their fingers as they unfolded the legs. Then we kids would help arrange the rest of our things. Each year we thought of ways to make it better.

"The arrangement I recall most clearly was with Mom's cot in the front on the right, the card table in the middle of the front, and on the left would be some board-and-concrete-block shelves or a small cupboard and the ice chest to make the kitchen area. On the back two floorboards of the tent we had our two cots on the right, one behind the other with a small space between, and on the left we put up a curtain and behind that our dresser and then another cot. The clothes were covered with a piece of fabric and hung on a pole in the middle of the back, separating the two cots on the right from the dresser and cot on the left. The tent front and back walls were flaps, and on really hot afternoons we opened all four as much as we could.

"The Soquel campground was a big place. As you drove in the main gate, the end of the main auditorium was just to your right. To the left of the auditorium, campers were parked in rows. Way down on the left there was a metal building for Sabbath School supplies and instruction classes, a fenced picnic area, and beyond that, a meadow with more campers. The auditorium was a huge Quonset-type of building. One time we were at the campground during the winter. I was amazed to see that all of the tents, rolled up and stacked on pallets, took up only one small corner of the huge building. Attached to the back of the auditorium, but with a separate entrance, was the ABC, and upstairs a lodge for the guest speakers. To the right of the main auditorium was another long building. It contained the cafeteria at the near end, the deli in the middle, where vegetarian burgers and corndogs were sold, and at the far end, the camp grocery store, where every year at the end of camp meeting Mom bought cases of Loma Linda® and Worthington® foods to last till the following year.

"To the right of the main entrance, around the edge of the campground was the Dorcas tent, where many interesting crafts, quilts I could never afford, and beanbags that we loved to toss up the tent sides, were sold. I can still smell the dusty scent of my beanbag. Huge army-green tents housing the children's divisions were in a row beyond the Dorcas tent. The tents for Cradle Roll and Kindergarten were the closest, followed by Primary and Juniors, with Earliteen at the end. Around the far end was the Spanish tent and beside that the Youth tent. All across the back of the campground, from behind the first section of campers to the Youth tent in the far back right, were tents on terraces. Up behind the campground was a big hill. We would hike to the top, where on sunny afternoons you could see the blue ocean.

"Mornings would start with a calm wake-up announcement heralded by four bell tones over the PA system. Mornings at Soquel were usually foggy and cool. Mom would get up and go to the early meeting, and when we got older we would too. It was not easy to crawl out of a warm sleeping bag, and as the week wore on, it got harder to wake up. We ate breakfast in our tent after the early-morning meeting, and you could hear others doing the same. During the ten o'clock morning meeting the fog would lift, and it would start to get hot. We would meet after the morning meeting for lunch, usually at the corndog stand, and then rest in the afternoon, go to the afternoon meeting, and play till supper. We usually ate supper in the cafeteria. After supper there was just enough time to get cleaned up for the evening meeting. It was usually the best attended.

"I especially remember when Steve Marshall and David Meeker were the speakers for the youth. They were such interesting speakers that all seats were taken, and adults were crowding around the edge of the tent. During the evening meeting, the fog would return, and it would get quite cool. Though it was hard to think of taking a jacket when you went to the meeting, you really missed one if you forgot it! Our tent was usually close by other friends of our family, and after the meeting we would gather in one of the tents in our "neighborhood" and drink hot cider while the adults talked. Dad had to work during the week, so he attended meetings only the first evening and on Sabbaths. At night a soothing bedtime announcement would come over the PA system, and it felt good to rest. During the first few days of sitting in meetings, my legs would ache from so much sitting.

"There were shower houses, a laundry house, and cook house in the middle of each of the tent areas.

The cook houses were warm places to gather on the foggy mornings. We tented on the flat area near the Spanish meeting tent, and in our cook house we could watch the Hispanic ladies cook. Occasionally we even enjoyed a taste. We got our water from faucets at the end of the tent rows. By the end of camp meeting the area around the faucets was muddy! In the laundry house my mom bathed my little brother in the laundry sink. I thought that was embarrassing. He was naked in front of all those people! In the shower houses, we always wore rubber thongs on our feet and were careful not to drop our stuff on the wet (to us kids "gross") floor. After showering we had to be careful if we wanted our feet to stay clean. At the beginning of camp meeting, the grass all over the campground would be green, but during the ten days of camp meeting, the campground grass dried up and all the nonpaved walkways became quite dusty. Mom would pour water on the grass in front of our tent every day to try to keep it green and to keep the dust down, but always by the end of the ten days it was dry and very dusty.

"Camp meeting at Soquel started on a Thursday night late in July and lasted for ten days, into the first of August. The first year I ever went, my older brother and I stayed overnight in my grandmother's tent. She was sharing it with another older lady from our church. Later, my two grandmothers would share a tent or one of the cabins for the elderly—even though my grandmothers were very different. I think they got along because one was very easy going.

"That first year I remember my maternal grandmother being worried we would get cold at night. She made us beds on the tent floor and put newspaper from under the edge of the bed up the side of the tent about six inches to close the gap between the floor boards and the tent side. I think she did other things to make it cozy too.

"In early years I loved to baby-sit. Outside the Cradle Roll tent there were tons of strollers. It was so grand to push babies around the campground in their strollers. I remember in particular a curly redhead and thought how I would like to have a red-haired baby someday. Now I have one.

"One year our division had us sell some raffle tickets to raise money to help send kids to summer camp. There were prizes for selling different amounts, and I wanted the clock radio. I remember mentioning it to one of the staff of our tent. And then I actually won it! I was so thrilled that I ran all the way back to our tent, yelling, 'Mom! Mom! I got it!' As I ran down the path in front of our tent row, I tripped on a clump of grass and landed out flat. That was embarrassing!

"Of course there was a spiritual dimension to camp meeting as well. I recall that most of the youth, when I was that age, did not have the meetings as their main focus at camp meeting. I did, so I found camp meeting lonely until I met some new friends. I am sure I made the matter known to my Lord, and I received a clear answer to prayer: the first weekend it was announced in the youth tent that a group would work together to put on a play—and anyone interested could participate. That year turned out to be my best camp-meeting year. We worked hard, prayed together about our project, and found all sorts of places to rehearse, including the counseling trailer and the beach. The young people in the group were strong Christians, into their Bibles, and just plain nice and fun to be with. We had a great time as we hung out together working on our parts, and we became lifelong friends.

"On Sabbath my family would gather with our friends in one of our tents for a potluck. We would sit on the cots and on folding chairs on the grass in front of the tent. That last Saturday night after the evening meeting, we would load up our car and trailer and leave in the dark in a cloud of dust with the rest of the crowd. It had been wonderful to be close to friends and come closer to Jesus during these ten days. We would all try to continue this closeness throughout the coming year, but would find again a need for renewal next year, as we always had."

Memories like these are surely what makes attending camp meeting such a special tradition. In addition to being wonderful opportunities for spiritual renewal, attending camp meeting offers opportunities for our children to have fun with family and friends. Camp-meeting experiences make lasting impressions that can bind children's hearts strongly to God and to their church. Someday soon I hope my children and I will get to spend the entire week at camp meeting.

(I do have a warning for those of you attending camp meeting with teens. Because my children are not yet teens, I'm not qualified to give advice from the perspective of a parent. But I do have the perspective of a wild teenager who attended camp meeting as a non-SDA. Positive spiritual and social aspects of camp meeting are readily available for teens. Unfortunately, some kids think of camp meeting only as a great opportunity to socialize in inappropriate ways. Drinking beer and attending movies are among two of my first camp-meeting experiences. My advice? Know where your teens are and what they're doing. All the kids I hung out with were Adventists.)

Chapter Eight

Witnessing

One of the most important aspects of the family, in my opinion, is that from it society is changed, for good or for ill. It isn't so much the outside things that influence the family, as whatever is inside the family influencing those outside things. Or at least it should be. Family should be a powerful force in this society. Parents uplifting children, children obeying parents, everyone working for the good of humanity. "The family relationship should be sanctifying in its influence. Christian homes, established and conducted in accordance with God's plan, are a wonderful help in forming Christian character. Families here should be a symbol of the great family above. Parents and children should unite in offering loving service to Him who alone can keep human love pure and noble."[1]

I'm one of those "I feel; therefore I do," people, so it is easy for me to be motivated by warm do-gooder feelings. These feelings prompt me into missionary service in my community. I suppose there's nothing inherently wrong with these feelings, but they stop short of the ideal motivation. What happens when I don't "feel"? Then, I don't do.

The Bible is clear: "love one another." Not just when we feel like it. Not just when we happen to think about it. All the time. In everything. In all ways. OK, now you're committed. Starting today you're going to devote part of your time to helping those who need your help. What about your kids? Anyone who has ever baked cookies with two small children "helping" in the kitchen knows that prep time is doubled and clean-up time is increased. Leaving children out, however, isn't the answer.

Children need to learn that their entire family helps other people. "In an effort to excuse themselves some say: 'My home duties, my children, claim my time and my means.' Parents, your children should be your helping hand, increasing your power and ability to work for the Master. Children are the younger members of the Lord's family. They should be led to consecrate themselves to God, whose they are by creation and by redemption. They should be taught that all their powers of body, mind, and soul are His. They should be trained to help in various lines of unselfish service. Do not allow your children to be hindrances. With you the children should share spiritual as well as physical burdens. By helping others they increase their own happiness and usefulness."[2]

Almost every month (with my "helpers") I cook dinner for a halfway house at which former prisoners live while readjusting to society. Part of the arrangement is that we must eat with the residents, which is fine. We go as a family, occasionally as two families since my friend Debbie helps to cook and sometimes has the evening free to accompany us. But don't suppose that this is always an easy, delightful adventure. It's not. But I believe in it. I believe in what they're trying to accomplish at the halfway house. And it exposes my children to people who are grateful for a second chance.

One day Josh was complaining about having to go eat at the halfway house that evening. My first gut reaction, I must confess, was, "How can you say that? Don't you know how important what we're doing is? It hardly affects you anyway; after all, we have to eat somewhere." You get the picture. But I didn't say that. I took a deep breath, flung out a prayer for wisdom and patience, and instead asked him why he thought we were cooking for the halfway house in the first place.

He thought it over for a while and then shrugged and said, "I dunno."

So, I told him. I told him the whole story about Jesus telling His followers how they helped Him. "I was hungry and you gave me something to eat, I was thirsty and you gave me something to drink, I was a stranger and you invited me in, I needed clothes and you clothed me, I was sick and you looked after me, I was in prison and you came to visit me" (Matthew 25:35, 36, NIV). When I finished he said, "You mean we're feeding Jesus?" He was pretty impressed with that and hasn't complained since.

"Reaching out" is second nature to me. My mom was always doing something for someone in need. She provided Easter "lamb" cakes and hotcross buns for neighbors, groceries for people down and out, entertainment for nursing home residents. The list goes on. Even today she helps others in numerous ways. She is a board member at the Samaritan House, a homeless shelter, where she serves on committees and works on their quarterly newsletter. Her church provides meals for Martha's Kitchen, a local soup kitchen, five weeks a year. She brought us up to care about other people. I hope I can instill that same sense of caring in my children.

Anyone who ever dreamed of being a missionary is in luck because the family unit is a missionary unit. It's not only our privilege, it's our sacred responsibility to be missionaries. "Not all can go as missionaries to foreign lands, but all can be home missionaries in their families and neighborhoods. There are many ways in which church members may give the message to those around them. One of the most successful is by living helpful, unselfish Christian lives. Those who are fighting the battle of life at great odds may be refreshed and strengthened by little attentions which cost nothing. Kindly words simply spoken, little attentions simply bestowed, will sweep away the clouds of temptation and doubt that gather over the soul. The true heart expression of Christlike sympathy, given in simplicity, has power to open the door of hearts that need the simple, delicate touch of the spirit of Christ."[3]

"Our youth group put on a banquet for the senior citizens of our church once. They had a three-course meal complete with table decorations and waiters in uniforms. They also provided transport for those who didn't have cars. It was much appreciated." –JUDI LARSEN, NEW ZEALAND

When my friend Peggy Harris was growing up, her family's primary outreach was to the Muckleshoot Tribe. "When I was a village student at Auburn

Adventist Academy, we started a sunshine band that was different from the traditional one. Since my mother had a clinic for the Muckleshoot Tribe in our home (which was surrounded by the reservation), we invited a group of students to go to neighboring homes to sing, pray, and read a scripture. Many times we could not all get into the tiny homes and would stand outside and sing. The Muckleshoots loved it.

"We also started a Sunday School for the Muckleshoot Tribe in a new building my parents had built behind our home. A teacher from Auburn Adventist Academy was our adult coordinator, and several students taught the lessons and did the program just like Sabbath School. Children came from all over the reservation to attend. We gave out *Our Little Friend*® papers to the children.

"On the Muckleshoot Reservation each year at Christmas time we held a big Christmas party in their community hall. Seattle Junior Academy would collect and repair toys that were sent out. Local businesses provided baby items, cookies, and fruit so that all the families attending received a gift from Santa Claus and had refreshments. The children from the Sunday School presented a program of songs they had learned.

"From these activities I learned early that even though I might not be able to go overseas as a missionary, there was always a mission at my door. Throughout my life I have found this to be true, wherever I live or work. There is great satisfaction in being able to share with and brighten someone else's life."

Children who grow up realizing that life does not revolve around them, that it's their responsibility to help others, have a better chance of making missionary work part of their grown-up lives. Susan M. Swayze was raised by her maternal grandparents, Hobart and Mary Webb. "My grandfather was the church elder," recalls Susan. "This was when a pastor had four or more churches. He'd rotate his Sabbaths so each congregation was lucky if they saw/heard him once a month. My grandfather preached more sermons to our congregation some years than the pastor did. Grandfather also had the midweek service every Wednesday night.

"He led out in Ingathering and was the church's unofficial maintenance man for as long as he was alive. My grandmother was church organist for over forty years, taught the Primary Sabbath School lesson for years, and attended the Dorcas Society faithfully every week.

"Their lives were wrapped up in their Troy (New York) SDA Church. I thought that was the way everyone lived! When I was a youngster I remember on Sabbath afternoons (probably a couple times a month), after we had dinner cleared away, my grandfather would get out all his supplies—pieces of white paper, rubber bands, and church papers: *Our Little Friend*®, *Review*, *Signs of the Times*®, pamphlets galore, you name it and it was there—and we would begin.

"First we'd place a piece of white paper down on the table, then put three or four of these church papers on top of the white paper and roll them together in one roll, put a rubber band around it, and stand it on end in a box. We would do this until the box was full. Then we'd get in the car, my grandmother in the front passenger seat and me in the back seat with our windows open. My grandfather would drive around the suburbs and rural residential areas while my grandmother and I tossed these 'treasures' out the window onto people's driveways or lawns.

"My grandfather may have thought this was a good Sabbath activity for a child. He was right. I may have been around eight or nine when we started this routine. I always enjoyed it and have never forgotten it, even if my childish goal was to see how far into the driveway I could throw the papers. I wish I had continued this practice with my children when they were little. I think they would have enjoyed it, too. My grandparents definitely raised me with the old-fashioned missionary spirit. To this day I frequently wonder how best to tell someone about my Jesus."

What I like about Susan's grandparents' ideas is that they made witnessing a part of their lives. They could have said that their church jobs took enough of their time and that they had no time left to witness. Instead, they included witnessing as part of their routine. When you begin to think about starting a family ministry, excuses will pop up faster than the popcorn on Saturday night. Most of the excuses are flimsy paper boats that will become soggy and sink. With God's guidance, you can find a ministry that is possible and appropriate for your family to do.

Location can't be used as an excuse because some ministries can be done without leaving home. The Hendricksons of Pendleton, Oregon, make their own cards for special occasions. "We believe letter writing and card making is a ministry!" Lora told me. "As a family we made and sent cards and prayed for two church members dying of cancer. We thought about them as a family and attended their funerals together too."

Ardie Earhart could use her husband as an excuse; he's not an Adventist. Or her children; they're not practicing any religious beliefs, which saddens her.

But, she doesn't. "Once a week, during the week, I visit or take a nursing-home resident for a wheelchair ride around the neighborhood. She used to attend our church. Her children live quite far away and cannot visit as often as they would like."

> "We are going this week to talk to the activity director at the local nursing home, go on a tour, meet some people. We are going to work on visiting once a week to sing for them. We may go a Sabbath or two a month, and every Tuesday afternoon for an hour. Our kids need to be little ministers! We sing for people because it is an encouragement for them, not because we want to perform or show off." –LORA HENDRICKSON

Ideally, the entire church should be involved in outreach in conjunction with the family. That may sound like a no-brainer, but you'd be surprised. I belonged to a church once where efforts to "get the entire church involved" with individual and family ministry met with little success. While the church supported the *idea* of ministry and encouraged the efforts of those individuals and families in *words*, the membership would not follow through with any tangible help. The people who started the minitries were left to carry them on single-handedly as best they could.

"We at our church have designated the second Sabbath of the month as 'Visiting Sabbath,' " says Larry Houtchens. "On these days we have a fellowship meal. Afterward, we visit shut-ins and missing members or sing at nursing homes and the hospital. Every time, the results are tears of joy, hearts touched, bridges built, bonds made, and a bit of heaven experienced."

Like the song says, "That's what it's all about."

Children like to be involved. When we cook for the halfway house, I let my kids help. Our efforts are applauded (literally), so why should I get all the credit? Mentioning their efforts always brings them special notice and appreciation. They feel like club members, not people on the outside looking in. I think this makes the biggest difference between kids who lose interest in projects like this (and for that matter, church activities in general) and kids who go on to have their own missionary projects. The kids who get involved have invested in the outcome.

"With us as parents and as Christians it rests to give our children right direction. They are to be carefully, wisely, tenderly guided into paths of Christlike ministry. We are under sacred covenant with God to rear our children for His service. To surround them with such influences as shall lead them to choose a life of service, and to give them the training needed, is our first duty."[4]

"One member of our church has made a list of all children of church members, at least younger members of their families, and given each of us willing to participate, two names to faithfully pray for each day." –Roy H. Steck

---

Family ministries are wonderful ways to involve children. They can participate as they are able in a loving, supportive environment. One family in Maine has several great family ministry traditions. (This family prefers to remain anonymous.)

"One tradition we have is a book club. We meet about five times a year and discuss a book together. We've read some terrific books and have learned a lot as we've shared what the books meant to us personally. This group is diverse. We have university professors, boat builders and designers, math teachers, and others. We eat a potluck supper first; then we sit around the fire and discuss the book.

"Inviting people who had experiences pertaining to the book added a depth and dimension to the discussion that was tremendous. We invite authors also (when possible). I chose books that were a great read (very interesting) and had something important to teach or impart. Some of the books were life-changing. Occasionally we choose a theme for the year, such as courage."

I find it interesting that this family doesn't choose overtly religious books for their club. This allows them to invite a much broader range of people, and, more important, people who could benefit the most from the group. Their emphasis on reading books with a good message would give them ample opportunity to discuss their life views with participants.

If you'd like to start a book club, here are some suggestions from the family in Maine who has used them:

Eastern Approaches by Sir Fitzroy MacLean
To War With Whitaker by the Countess of Ranfurly
(Previous two may not be of such general interest but were great.)
The Rebel Yell and the Yankee Hurrah by John Haley
Coastal Maine by Roger Duncan
Faithful Travelers by James Dodson
The Long Walk by Slavomir Rawicz (EXCELLENT)
Life and Death in Shanghai by Nien Cheng (EXCELLENT)

Endurance by Alfred Lansing (Excellent, and there are more books about this story such as *The Endurance* by Caroline Alexander.)
Man's Search for Meaning by Viktor Frankl (Outstanding)

No matter which activity your family chooses to witness to others, by far your greatest influence is how you live out your daily life. Strengthen your family unit at the altar of God so He can work through you to change the lives of those around you. Be a shining light in the darkness of the world.

---

1. *Signs of the Times,* Ellen G. White, September 6, 1899.
2. *The Adventist Home,* Ellen G. White, pp. 485, 486.
3. Ibid., p. 485.
4. Ibid., p. 484.

Chapter Nine

Family Vacations

Family vacations are very important. Just ask me. We've taken one for the past two years, and I have to wonder why we waited so many years to take the first one. Of course, family vacations tend to get a bad rap. Supposedly, kids and travel don't mix well.

It warmed my heart to see how many of you enjoy my personal favorite vacation: camping. As I was growing up, my family did a great deal of hiking and camping—and those times are among my most cherished memories. My husband and I take our own children canoe camping. We call our canoe the *No Bananas* after the old song "Yes, We Have No Bananas"; we both agree that the canoe has been one of our best investments.

Certainly taking time as a family away from everyday duties is both a necessity and a joy. Busy families, even ones who make time together a priority, still need to spend "just us" time. Ellen White tells us, "They should have a change frequently, should often devote a day wholly to recreation with their families, who are almost entirely deprived of their society."[1] She was probably referring to fathers who had indoor jobs and were away from home most of the day, but today her statement can apply just as much to mothers—and sometimes to busy children.

Choices of vacation activities and locations vary from family to family. Not only does it depend greatly on the family members' interests, but on budget and distance considerations, as well. Our young children (ages four and seven) travel well for about two hours, which limits our travel radius. We'll occasionally push it to four hours, but have never gone beyond that. On the other hand, family friends with children as young as ours drove across the United States. It all depends on what your children are able to do.

Overnight hiking, while a fabulous activity, is better enjoyed by older children, which is why we use the canoe for our camping. Perhaps later (when the children can carry their own packs), we'll do some overnight backpacking trips with them as well. Before you decide what kind of vacation to take, spend a little time analyzing your family's interests and abilities.

"The best thing for our family has been hiking together," Elizabeth Howe told me. "For several years we have worked on the goal of climbing as many state highpoints together as we can. I'm sure this is not for everyone (and it can get costly, but plain old hiking doesn't need to be). But we've enjoyed it because it's out-of-doors, good for our health, gives lots of time for interaction (or there is room for going at your own rate, i.e., teenagers like to leave us adults in the dust), and there are opportunities for helping each other obtain our goal. We have even needed each other to stay alive. It's been an activity that our kids are proud of.

"Whenever we go on a trip to visit relatives, we check whether there is a state highpoint along the way and plan to visit it. We have also planned a couple summer trips just to climb highpoints. We have done almost thirty, including the hardest ones in the lower forty-eight (not Mount Rainier and Mount Hood). Thank goodness there are still lots of easy ones to do, so I don't have to quit working on the list yet. It's also been a fun type of 'geography lesson.' Since I've home-schooled for thirteen years, I try to think about these things!"

Of course, you don't have to struggle to the top of a high peak to get together outside. You don't even have to use a tent. Rosalia Coffen's family goes camping in style—in a trailer.

"Vacation time was usually spent in nature," she says. "We visited some museums and amusement parks, but we always camped, mostly in a twelve-foot trailer. It was not until our boys were in their teens that we got a twenty-three-foot trailer. Those last few years, their computers had to go with us. But bringing the computers made our sons willing to spend a few more summers sharing vacations with us.

"Our older son's college graduation gift was a one-week vacation with us, most of it in nature. He continued to share our yearly vacations for another six years until he married. Our younger son joined the three of us on a trip to the Canadian Rockies for his college graduation gift."

One of the great things about camping—besides being inexpensive, accessible, and downright fun—is that you can do it with a hundred of your friends.

Well, nearly. A few years ago my side of the family began to meet once a year at Lake Carmi, in northeastern Vermont. We had so much fun the second year that we decided to do it twice a year, and we still do. The atmosphere is relaxing, meal responsibility is divided up so no one person does all the cooking and washing up, and the kids are so busy catching polliwogs and crawfish on the shore (which is in clear

TINFOIL DINNERS

These make easy and delicious camping fare.
—Submitted by Crystal Watt, who remembers fondly summer camping with her family in the Adirondacks.

2 cups vegetables, peeled and diced
   (suggestions: carrots, potatoes, onions, green peppers, squash, broccoli)
1 or 2 tablespoons butter or olive oil (to keep the vegetables from sticking to the foil)
1/2 cup meat substitute (we use chopped Morningstar® Breakfast Links®)
Salt and other seasonings to taste (garlic powder is great)
(These ingredients serve one person. Multiply to suit your need.)

Lay a double layer of heavy-duty foil on a table. Place all ingredients in a pile and wrap them carefully in the foil. Your campfire should be hot, at the red-coal stage. Avoid putting the dinners in the fire; place them on a grate. Depending on how full your aluminum envelopes are, they should take 30 to 60 minutes to bake. Rotate and flip them every 10 to 15 minutes. Serve right in the foil, crinkled like a bowl for easy clean-up. *This recipe tastes great at home during the winter too—and really brings back those summer memories.*

sight of the lean-to) that they collapse into their sleeping bags at night. If you have children, you'll know just what a miracle that is. These two camping trip/family reunions are greatly anticipated throughout the year.

You can take vacations with friends too, which we sometimes do, though they are usually not as well planned. The Culbertsons believe in playing hard while camping. "We tent camp," Donita says. "It is inexpensive, but does require preplanning for food though. We often meet relatives and/or friends at a campground within one or two hours' travel from our home. This works great for holidays or just a weekend. We take a croquet game and table games (Uno™, Pass the Pig). We even have invented our own, i.e., the hatchet toss. The Powder Puffs (gals) actually won once. S'mores ingredients are a must for campfire fun. We've been tubing in the river, taken bikes, and even worked on scrapbooks. What we do depends on the group and where we go. Even teens are rarely bored out in nature."

Of course, to enjoy nature you don't have to put up with rustic conditions if you don't want to. You can attend a family camp, which, is usually less primitive.

"For ten years running we have attended family camp at Camp Ida-Haven in McCall, Idaho," Donita told me. "The meals, cabin, waterfront activities, horseback riding, challenge course, worships, etc. are included. That's MY idea of a vacation! My son was baptized there. What wonderful memories we have. We make our reservations each January."

The Culbertsons are my heroes. These folks are serious about their vacations. "We took a month and drove 6,000 miles through twelve states to see family and friends," says Donita. "We tried to stay with them whenever possible to cut costs. We ate out (while on the road) once daily. We got fresh fruit/veggies and sandwich stuff at stores for the other meals. The kids each wrote ('encouraged' by Dad) in a journal five minutes daily. We took tons of Adventures in Odyssey tapes. These stories kept us sane and provided good moral fun at the same time. I often get a new set of tapes for each long trip, and we all enjoy them!"

"When we head out on a long car journey, we make sure that we have a book to read aloud or tapes to listen to." –Kathy Phillips

---

To go almost anywhere and camp, you still come up against the boredom of a long drive. Tapes go a long way to alleviate that. We use them as well. Be sure to stock up because although children don't mind listening to the same one over and over, adults will be ready to drive off a bridge. Many creative people have invented car games you can play to actually have fun while traveling. Laurie Murphy is one of these people.

"On outings or errands, we look for old VW bugs and vans. New ones don't count. The first one to see it, calls it. He or she then is allowed a 'slug.' 'Slugs' may not hurt and may take the form of tickles, hugs, or kisses. Various rules have developed over time—a car can be called only once in a trip (for a parked car and one you see coming and going), you can't save your 'slugs'—they need to be used that trip, don't 'slug' the driver, Vanagans® don't count—only the older ones. Some rules have been tried and rejected, such as, vans were worth two, convertibles were worth more. The child allowed in the front seat of the van is rotated, unless we are in a vehicle with an airbag; then no one under twelve is allowed up front. If we get out of the vehicle, the turn to sit in the front seat rotates, even if we have only walked across a parking lot."

Tape Sources

The Quiet Hour (character-building and historical tapes) 909-793-2588

Focus on the Family (Adventures in Odyssey and other tapes) 1-800-A FAMILY

If children learn a little something while traveling, all the better. Sandra Cruz has come up with learning games to keep kids occupied while traveling. "For stress-free vacations, take some new books with you that they haven't seen. These can come from the library. Three books per child is the limit.

"Teach children to read the road map, and put them, one at a time, in charge of telling everyone 'where we are.' Let them know where the trip ends. Give them math problems to solve using the numbers you see along the highway. Play alphabet with road signs, license plates, truck ads, or all of these. Personal tape players are nice for peace and quiet, but no good for socializing. Resist putting music or sermons you like in the car tape deck. Buy children a treat once in a while—like an ice cream cone—even if it's not particularly healthful. That is what they will remember most about the vacation. Buy them inexpensive cameras and film, and let them take pictures to remember their vacation."

Cameras are fascinating to young children. We used to buy Josh the disposable kind. Just recently some friends gave him a children's camera they had outgrown. It's interesting to see what kids take pictures of. "If you want to know what children are interested in," my friend Darren Manzari says, "just give them a camera. At first you'll get lots of pictures of nothing, but once they get over the novelty, they start to take pictures of the things that really appeal to them—and you'll get a sense of what's important to them."

"And you'll get to see what you look like first thing in the morning with bed hair," his wife Nancy laughs.

Stopping for a treat now and then is a great idea too. It makes the journey more of an adventure than a torture to be endured. As a child I always suffered from motion sickness, which probably explains my aversion to traveling even today. Two things helped: stopping now and then and having something to snack on.

Any time you spend doing an activity can be considered a family vacation, even if it's only a couple hours on a Sunday. Joshua remarked recently, "We need to have more family time." He was right. We'd been very busy finishing our home-school year. So we joined the Green Mountain Club as a family. This Sunday we'll go on our first hike together with the group on a Children's Adventure Series Hike. Chances are, if you inquire, you'll find lots of these opportunities for a mini family vacation in your town.

No matter what you do together as a family for vacation, you can be sure that the memories you create will last your children, and you, a lifetime. I firmly believe that no one will ever look back on their life and say, "Wasn't that a great movie we saw?" or "Say, wasn't it great working so much?" Rather, it will be the quiet moments by the campfire or on the boat or the fun during a game that will be remembered and cherished. Those are the *true* family traditions.

---

1. *My Life Today,* Ellen G. White, p. 206.

Chapter Ten

Family Worship

Family worship is one of the easiest family traditions to establish and slipperiest family tradition to maintain. It requires no fancy equipment to get started. All you need is a family who is willing to pray together. It's slippery because life, under the manipulation of Satan, often contrives to keep us from this simple, powerful family tradition.

Our family worship has worn many faces. Most recently it is fragmented. We have prayer before my husband leaves for work and the children and I begin school. Our curriculum involves a study of Christianity, reading the Bible, and memorizing Scripture, which qualifies as worship to me. I have a picture in my mind of what family worship should look like, and though our family doesn't conform to that picture, I have to conclude that in the end it doesn't matter what your family worship looks like. The important part is that you worship God together as a family.

"We always had family worship together," says Kimberly Harris. "It included a story from *The Bible Story* series, prayer during which everyone had the opportunity to pray, followed by a theme song that we all sang, even though none of us except the baby could carry a tune."

When Joshua was a toddler, we'd sing through all the Cradle Roll songs. I'm not sure why we stopped. It was probably due to morning sickness I endured while I carried his sister. Singing is usually confined now to sundown worship. But, it's something I'd like to incorporate more. Singing seems to be important to our sense of "worship."

When Joshua was small, I even bought one of those gigantic felt sets (I'm still cutting those figures out) so that I could use them for worship. He loved putting the felts on the felt board. If I had it to do over again, I'd sure look for a set already cut out! You might be fortunate enough to get some supplies for family worship from people who worked in the children's departments, like Rosalia did.

"When she quit working in the children's Sabbath School departments, my mother-in-law gave us all the Sabbath School activity things she had used," Rosalia Coffen told me. "For many years, when our sons were preschoolers, evening worship was a mini Sabbath School.

"When the boys were in the lower grades, I read *The Desire of Ages* to them, one page each morning while they ate their breakfast. We would always talk about what we read. No one objected, and they often had something to contribute to the discussion. Morning worships continued to be part of the breakfast scene through academy. There was never a problem with that.

"Some of our most precious times as a family were the discussions we had with our worships. Our evening worships, as the boys got older, were often books written by such authors as Philip Yancey and Lewis Smedes. They lent themselves to discussions, usually started by my husband. It seemed to help our sons learn how to think about God and the Bible—to learn how to think for themselves."

Sometimes it seems that the big flashes of insight make the most difference, but that's not true. It's usually in the quiet moments of discussion that real character is formed and truths are taught. In answering our children's questions and talking them through their concerns, we become trusted partners in the journey of life. Taking time for the little things gives us the right to offer help with the big things later on.

"We do try hard to have morning and evening worship, much thanks to my husband," Elizabeth Howe told me, "but we don't do anything special besides having it. Right now we are reading through Psalms in the morning. We read a chapter a day, reading the verses around in a circle. In the evening we read books such as *Mere Christianity*, *Adventist Review* articles, or biographies of famous Christians. We used to sing a lot when our guitarist son, Evan, was around. One other thing we like to do is read the responsive readings from the back of the hymnal. We read until we get to a punctuation mark and then it's the next person's turn. It's really fun to do it that way."

There are thirty-one chapters in Proverbs, which make it a great book for worship readings. Just find the chapter that matches the date. The Proverbs won't leave you hanging, but many families are fans of reading chapter books for worship. Kids become keenly interested in what will happen next, and their interest is easily maintained. Uncle Arthur, is, of course, a popular reading choice for worship.

It's never too early to start thinking about family worship. "My husband and I are planning to start a tradition in our family with the birth of our child in January," Julie Voth says. "For our first child we had a prayer of dedication immediately after the birth at the first possible moment of quiet 'family time.' We are planning to expand this tradition at the birth of our next child by also singing the beautiful blessing from Michael Card's Sleep Sound in Jesus CD—the one based on the passage in Numbers that states, "The Lord bless you and keep you; the Lord make his face shine upon you and be gracious to you; the Lord turn his face toward you and give you peace" (Numbers 6:24-26, NIV).

"What a wonderful thing—to dedicate your child from the very first moment and to bind each member of a family together in God's peace. We also end each night's worship by singing the chorus of 'Wonderful Peace,' which begins, 'Peace! peace! wonderful peace.' It helps our little people know it's time to sleep and sends them there in the peace of God."

My friend Anita Jacobs told me about the special family worship tradition that now encompasses her children's families. "We started this Jacobs family tradition when our children were young. Somewhere, and I don't remember where, I heard this variation of the song 'Blest Be the Tie That Binds':

Blest be the tie that binds
Our hearts in Jesus' love.
The fathers, the mothers, the sisters, the brothers.
And lead us to heaven above.

"After worship and prayer each evening, we would kneel in a circle (we have three children) and sing this song. When we came to 'the fathers,' my husband Frank would sing that part; I would sing 'the mothers'; our daughter 'the sisters'; and our two sons 'the brothers.' Then we'd all join together in 'And lead us to heaven above.'

"Now the children are grown and our sons both have children, so they are the fathers and the brothers! Our daughter just had her first baby, so she'll join with the mothers.

"Each year we have a Jacobs family gathering at Myrtle Beach, where we rent a large house for a week. We have a wonderful time, but probably one of the highlights is when we gather for evening worship and sing together. And we always close after prayer with the song mentioned above. Since most of us sing, we have some wonderful harmonies. Now it's the grandchildren who sing about the brothers and sisters. It's always a big deal when they can sing their part."

"Here are some things my kids enjoy doing for worship: dressing up and acting out a Bible story or character for me to guess, choosing a song or story, drawing a picture to illustrate their favorite Bible story, and taking turns being 'in charge' of worship." –JUDI LARSEN, NEW ZEALAND

Family worship will evolve as your family grows and changes. A family with small children won't have the same style of worship as a family with teens.

"We have family worship, morning and evening," Lora Hendrickson says. "Our evening worship ends with prayer, everyone kneeling in a circle holding hands. We sing a prayer song, then pray one at a time, starting with the youngest and ending with Dad or our guests, if we have some. (If we have cousins visiting, they pray in reverse age order as pre-assigned before we start our prayer.) Everyone knows what to do and when he or she is to do it. Some continuity is great.

"Our worships aren't 'exciting,' but the kids love them. We sing, read, play the 'emotions' game, etc. The kids love to charade emotions, and it gives us a great chance to talk about embarrassment, jealousy, and other emotions kids experience. We are learning to sing in parts; sometimes singing is all we do for worship. Lately we have been reading an interesting nature devotional."

Having regular family worships is a powerful means of drawing family members closer to each other and closer to the Lord. He is the unseen Guest at every family worship, eager to strengthen and bless each member of the family. He supports you in establishing this most important of family traditions.

CHAPTER ELEVEN

MISCELLANEOUS

Some traditions that readers submitted fit into no major category but are too good to not include. This eclectic chapter is stuffed with neat little goodies you'll want to add to your own list of traditions.

Everyone has stacks of pictures to deal with. When we started having children, the rolls of film began to pile up. I have pictures in stacks that would give serious competition to the Statue of Liberty. I love Ernie Medina's tradition for dealing with all those photos.

"My wife Keri and I have had this tradition since we've been married," Ernie Medina, Jr., told me. "We both love photography, having averaged about a roll a week for the last ten years. Every time we process a roll, we set aside 'contenders' for this year's collage. Then at the end of the year, during Christmas vacation, we go through the envelope full of contenders—highlights of the past year—and winnow them down to the final twenty or so that make the year's collage.

"On our wall, we have nine collages of highlights from each of the years we've been married, and it's a great reminder as we walk by them in the hall to look back and see the past years. Much easier than pulling out all of our albums! This has been one of our most consistent traditions—and one that family and friends enjoy looking at when they visit, especially when they find themselves making the 'collage wall.'

"When we were first married, we lived in an apartment for a few years but knew we had to move out of it before we ran out of hallway wall space for each year's collage! Now we live in a two-story house, and we're slowly filling up all the wall space along the stairway and at the top of the stairs. The space should last for a few more years."

In our family we have a little tradition we call the "Love Cups." Rob and I learned this tradition at a Caring For Marriage weekend we spent at the home of our friends Joe and Deloris Foote. The "Love Cup," in this case a mug with a cute Adirondack picture on it, is left somewhere obvious and filled on the sly by either spouse. We liked it so well that each of the kids now have their own mugs too.

"Thirteenth Sabbath programs are a tradition," my friend Trudy Morgan-Cole informs me. "Especially with the very little kids who are supposedly going to sing 'Jesus Loves Me' but stand there either giggling or frozen with fright while the mothers do the actual singing (I've now been on BOTH sides of this!).

"Footwashing has to be the ultimate Adventist tradition in the sense of being almost unique to the denomination. (The great cultural shift that occurred during my childhood was when women went from washing barefoot to leaving on their stockings—related, I'm sure, to the shift from stockings to pantyhose. I recall dimly the early days when women had begun wearing pantyhose but still thought they should take them off for the ordinance—as it was then called—the shimmying and shaking that went on until some brave soul decided the symbolism was just as effective if she left her pantyhose on!

"Now it always seems mildly indecent to me if I glance into the men's side of the room and see all those naked feet! In fact, I feel horribly uncomfortable looking into the men's side at all during footwashing. Occasionally I have to play the piano while both men and women sing. A curtain separates the two groups, but the piano is on the men's side, and I hate going over there to play it. Foortwashing is really a very primitive ritual when you think about it. My dad always thought it should be updated, for example, people could shine each other's shoes or something. Still humbling, but useful."

"I was talking with my youth group the other day about 'generic Adventist punch'—the beverage served at potlucks and socials. Five or six different flavors of frozen juice are combined with lemon-lime soda or ginger ale. The combination is an odd red or, worse, brown color. To me it's a classic." —TRUDY J. MORGAN-COLE

One of those unmistakable signs of growing up—the kind that make me cry—is the children's baby teeth coming out. It's just so traumatic, so final. Kids, of course, love it. At first Josh was willing to put his tooth under his pillow when I promised his father or I would sneak in and replace it with money, but eventually we had to just leave the money with nothing in exchange. He decided teeth were much too interesting to give up, even for money.

We always leave money, but I like Laurie Murphy's idea better. "The tooth fairy is one of our traditions. The 'tooth fairy' looks for the tooth (in an envelope with name and date written by the child) and leaves a book."

Laurie Murphy also makes a "memory box," a collection of childhood memories. I thought I invented that idea! "Each of our children has a memory box. It's a cardboard box that stores a select number of childhood things—a newspaper from the day the child was born, along with a couple of magazines, a favorite outfit (Mom thing), favorite toy, report cards, ticket stubs from a special outing. Only Mom or Dad can add to the box, or it would be full of their 'must have's.' The children have their own memory boxes in their rooms, which they are in charge of. The lid has to be able to close; the old must make way for the new."

I also love the special ways we decorate our homes, inside and out. Some of us get more creative in the outside department. I manage a few flowerbeds and some wind chimes, but Jeannie Fehl has a really unique idea.

"We always have a sign of some kind hanging outside of the house to welcome whoever is coming to visit or just coming home from being away," she says. "We did finally spray paint on a sheet a general Welcome, and then would hang it up outside and add something to it to specialize it for that person."

Celebrating life is one thing, but it's hard to get used to separation and death being a part of life. We try to ignore it as long as possible, but at some point it touches each of us directly. LeAnne Cornforth-Crawford's tradition touched my heart. I hope this affirming tradition catches on and spreads.

"A few years ago my husband's roommate from Thunderbird Adventist Academy passed away," LeAnn told me. "At his funeral we spent time with his family, the Vegaras, talking about the good memories. Ricki and Eddie mentioned that when a family member would have to leave after a visit, they would stand and hold up one finger pointing upward until that family member would drive out of view. This finger pointing to heaven meant, 'God be with you. We love you. And if we don't see you again on this earth, we will see you when Christ comes again.'

"After the funeral we were headed out the driveway to catch our plane home, and we saw their family standing in front of the door all pointing toward heaven. It was a wonderful way to say goodbye to those we love. At this same time my mother-in-law, Genny Crawford, had just been diagnosed with terminal lung cancer. It hit us all pretty hard, so we decided to visit her and Dad. They knew Vince and the Vegara family well, and we told them all about our trip to attend Vince's funeral. When we told them about the special goodbye, we realized that this was a tradition we needed to share with our family as well.

"As we drove away after that first trip of many, Mom and Dad both stood on their front porch, pointing toward heaven until we drove out of sight. And we, in turn, held our hands out the car windows pointing upward until we rounded the corner. Mom had almost two more years with us. She had such a wonderful relationship with God that she had peace in the midst of her storm until she went to sleep in

Christ. I will never forget how after her funeral they put her casket into the white hearse, and we all stood as she was driven away to the mortuary.

"Without a word, the hands of Dad, us kids, grandkids, sisters, brothers, and church family all raised and pointed upward as we had come to know this wonderful tradition. For one last time we got to say, 'Mom, God be with you. We love you. And the next time we see you will be when Christ comes.' It's a promise we plan to keep and a tradition we plan to pass on."

"Everything about Pathfinders is an Adventist tradition. Especially camporee—not your big slick Oshkosh-style camporee, but the humble local camporee at the conference campgrounds. I vividly recall an activity in which we had to light a fire, then try to cook pancakes over it without any real utensils like a frying pan or anything, then scraping the barely warm, congealed dough off this stick and attempting to eat it. It must have been a competition. I would never have done it if we weren't trying to beat the guys.

"Oh, and good-conduct awards at the end of the year, which my two friends and I always prided ourselves on never getting. There were four girls in our unit, and one always got a good-conduct award, and the rest of us made up for her."
—Trudy Morgan-Cole

Gwen Simmons shared her first-snow-day tradition with me. Considering we have many snow days in Vermont and could use a positive spin on the stuff,

I think I'll put this one into practice next winter.

"I'm not sure how it started," she confessed, "but each year here in Iowa, our family designates the first day of snow as 'fudge day'! Now it can't be just flurries. Those don't count. It has to be a 'real' snow—you know, big, fluffy flakes that keep coming down until the ground is covered. The ground must be covered—or no fudge. Then when we're sure it's a 'real' snowstorm, we get out the ingredients and make the fudge recipe from my own childhood. There is some-

Gwen's First-Snow-of-the-Year Fudge

1 cube butter
1 5-ounce can evaporated milk
1 tablespoon water
1 tablespoon corn syrup
2 cups sugar
4 tablespoons cocoa
1 tablespoon vanilla

In a medium saucepan, melt butter. Add milk, water, and corn syrup; slowly stir in sugar and cocoa until smooth. Bring to boil. Allow to gently boil until it reaches the firm soft ball stage*. Add vanilla; remove from heat. Stir vigorously in pan until it begins to lose its shine. Pour into a buttered dish. (If you like nuts, add them when adding the vanilla.) Allow to cool completely before cutting.

* To determine "firm soft ball stage," drop about a teaspoon of boiling fudge into a cup of cold water. If it has boiled long enough, the liquid fudge will gather into a firm ball. If it doesn't, it needs to boil longer. If it cracks, it has boiled too long. It may need to be tested several times.

thing quite special, and quite traditional in this house, about snowy windows and the smell of bubbling fudge on the stove."

As Adventists we may tend to place a bit more emphasis on food than the average citizen. (Do you agree?) Cookbooks are valued items. How are you ever going to make the loaf again if you lose your cookbook? I love Penny Estes Wheeler's idea of jotting notes in the cookbook to turn it into a journal of sorts. Her cookbooks aren't just valuable; they're family heirlooms.

"Since I was first married, I've made notes next to recipes I've used for the family," Penny shared with me. "At first they were cryptic: 'Burns easily; watch carefully,' or 'OK, not great.' Later I added the date and the occasion for which it was made: church potluck; Gerald's thirtieth birthday; Valentine's Day, and so forth. Then I began including brief notes on what was happening in our lives on the day it was made. Many entries document family celebrations—our teens' class parties, mission trips, a college student leaving for overseas, or beginning a new job.

"Over the years we had kids in four time zones. Sometimes I even noted where and what was happening in each of their lives when I made a favorite dish. What's especially gratifying to me is that now our adult children are making the same kind of notes in their cookbooks."

The writer in me gets all fired up with ideas like these. Penny carries her jotting over into traveling too. "For years I've kept a written log when I travel," she says, "especially when taking a car trip. And for years my kids have teased me about it, groaning and moaning as I jotted a reference to this fifteen-minute potty break or described something we'd just passed. When my father-in-law died suddenly in Michigan, our two youngest children, living in Texas, called and told us they were coming to the funeral. It was January, the weather iffy, and they were 1,000 miles away. 'Don't come!' I told them, even though they were both young adults. 'I don't want you to risk it.'

" 'We're coming,' they told me. 'We'll be there in time for the funeral.'

"And so they were, arriving minutes before it started.

"Afterward I couldn't help but laugh when I picked up the notebook I found in the front seat of Bronwen's car. '12:00 midnight,' her younger brother had written. 'Crossing the Mississippi River.' Then I could almost hear them laughing as I read, 'Mommy's probably awake right now wondering where we are!'

"They know me well!"

Her idea reminds me of the logbooks you see in lean-tos on the Long Trail, the hiking trail that runs the length of Vermont. It's always entertaining to see what other people were doing when they stayed at the shelter and to record what's going on during your own trip. Somehow, committing an event to paper makes it live longer.

I've not heard too many traditions for new members, so I was delighted to receive Peggy Harris's tradition. "We have often invited new members either to our home for dinner or at a luncheon at church when they joined our church by transfer or baptism," she told me. "We like to invite the pastor and his family to help them get acquainted with new members. When I was fellowship dinner coordinator at church, we would plan a new member fellowship dinner about twice a year so that new members could meet together with long-time members and the pastoral staff. They would then be invited to join a fellowship dinner team if they had not already done so."

I think that is a wonderful way to embrace new members and help them get comfortable in their new church home. Helen Burtnett's church has a special tradition as well. "When we moved to a new location, our church membership was transferred to the Deltona, Florida, SDA Church. The day we were voted in, we were placed in a 'parish group.' A woman had been assigned to phone and ask about our family, so on the Sabbath that we became members, she gave a two-paragraph biography, then had us stand, and our parish group leader (an elder) presented us with a lovely gift bag containing a pictorial church directory, a Roger Morneau book on prayer (which we already had, but it was a nice gift), a loaf of homemade bread, and a welcome card.

"Although I have been an Adventist since birth sixty-eight years ago, I had never seen this done before. I think it is a delightful gesture. It is hard to put into words the feeling of welcome and belonging that it produced, but I would recommend that the gift is worth the effort and cost. We have been members at that church for a year, and I enjoy hearing about others as they join our church. It rather breaks the ice for them too."

The final tradition I leave you with is Sabbath School Investment. While I recognize this instantly as an Adventist tradition, I can't say it is currently a vital one, which is a shame. I was always intrigued by the little I knew about Investment. I tried a few projects myself off and on, but there was never much motivation on the church level. I'd love to see this tradition revived. I think it could be a tremendous blessing.

Thurman C. Petty, Jr., wrote the book *I've Seen Miracles: A How-to Story Book of Sabbath School Investment.* This is an excellent resource to get you started if you are interested in reviving this tradition. "I feel that we've left out Sabbath School Investment in the church and in the home," Thurman told me. "It's become almost unknown in many places although it teaches the importance of missions and gives members a wonderful way to come into a close relationship with God."

Creating, reviving, and exploring traditions develop our relationship with God and strengthen that connection. Traditions cement our earthly relationships too. Whether you are just beginning to establish your family traditions or simply feel your traditions could use an energizing shot in the arm, I hope you have learned from people in these pages who have generously shared their time and traditions with us. Thank you once again to everyone who participated in the creation of this book. You are an inspiration to us all. May God use your creativity to inspire others and draw us all closer to Him.

Recipe Index

Carrot Tofu 56
Cheese Biscuits 39
Cheese Dip 74
Chocolate Fondue 75
Cottage Cheese Loaf 54
Fruit Crumble 61
Fudge 137
German Lasagna 63
Hashbrown Casserole 55
Lentil Soup 33
"Meatballs" 65
Oyster Cracker Snacks 77
Playdough Dessert 76
Potato Salad 59
Potato Soup 38
Sweet-and-Sour Dip 75
Tacos 32
Tinfoil Dinners 119
Waffles 37